The Merrill Studies
in
Second Skin

Compiled by

John Graham

University of Virginia

Charles E. Merrill Publishing Company
A Bell & Howell Company
Columbus, Ohio

For Albert Guerard who led the way

CHARLES E. MERRILL STUDIES

Under the General Editorship of
Matthew J. Bruccoli and Joseph Katz

ISBN: 0-675-09496-8

Library of Congress Catalog Card Number: 71-160518

1 2 3 4 5 6–76 75 74 73 72 71

Printed in the United States of America

Preface

In the early fifties Albert Guerard, then at Harvard, offered "English 166: Forms of the Modern Novel." Both "modern" and "forms" took on new meaning as we started with Flaubert and moved through Zola, Conrad, Joyce, Kafka, Dos Passos, Hemingway, West, Faulkner, Ennio Flaiano, and John Hawkes. In an enormous class, housed only by an auditorium, we found a subtle critic, an active novelist, and an eager teacher introducing the varieties of large and small skills of the novelist who creates a world.

Fortunately we had learned to trust him before he praised extravagantly a chunky orange-bound volume, *The Cannibal.* This unknown blew us apart. We did not have any idea from our cheap knowledge of little magazine "experimental writing" what a modern work of art could be.

We pursued or followed Hawkes through *Charivari* (1949), *The Cannibal* (1949), *The Beetle Leg* (1951), *The Goose on the Grave* and *The Owl* (1954), and *The Lime Twig* (1961). But the knowledge of one novel hardly prepared us for another in any way except that each demanded we abandon all predispositions and submit ourselves to the elements of fictional worlds that in some way, perhaps inexplicably, overwhelmed us. In *Second Skin* (1964) we found ourselves in the natural place of the imagination, not in fictionalized versions of the actual islands of Vinalhaven and Grenada. Hawkes does not place us easily in Hemingway's Paris, Pamplona, or Bimini; Fitzgerald's Little Egg or Cote d'Azur; or even Faulkner's Yoknapatawpha. He does something very different, more wonder filled, and yet just as real. We recognize places and events because we know Spenser's *The Faerie Queene,* a world in which anything can happen, and, without surprising us, does.

Just as the imaginative world of *Second Skin* is unique, the characters do not yield readily to analysis of consistent "motivation" although they sometimes have the simple force of minor gods and goddesses. Critics quite rightly turn immediately to the "voice" of Skipper, a voice which determines our vision of all. He is, in fact, an "ancient mariner" who has discovered love and must speak of it. But what of Miranda, Cassandra, Pixie, Sonny, Kate, and the dark captain and crew of the *Peter Poor*—or the *USS Starfish*? They press constantly on Skipper and seem, in spite of their simple functions, rather like Pearl of Hawthorne's *The Scarlet Letter* who radiates as the sun or reflects as the moon. How is their vividness gained, how do they function at any given point? Do they live only in Skipper's voice or are they as forcefully independent as they seem to be?

The style of *Second Skin* needs much more examination. Albert Guerard in his "The Prose Style of John Hawkes" (*Critique,* VI [1963], 19-29), emphasizes "the relative abandonment of 'literary' display," "the appeals of irony and control," and "voice" while noting recurrences of imagery, the positioning of adjectives and "the effects of abrupt or modulative transitions." All of these leads need further and particular exploration as do Hawkes' own statements on "fictional landscape," "distance" or "coldness," and "savage or saving comic spirit." Perhaps the ultimate question, still tied to "style," is precisely what is meaning of "comic" that can be derived from *Second Skin.*

Implicitly the style is examined through any concern with Skipper since it is Skipper's voice we hear as he attempts to sort out his life, to set down in his lover's language and cadence what has happened to him. Or to label his experiences so that he can endure the facts. The shifting narrative, the leaps between present and past, so richly stated, are his memory seeking an order and a value. But he is telling a story he thinks he knows and is plying the narrator's art of a Boswell who must pretend, while knowing the conclusion, that all is confused expectancy and experience. This book is what Skipper must and can live with. The tale is, however, ultimately an artifact, and questions remain for each particular shift: why did Hawkes place this event, this bit of information *here*? What are the effects of his juxtaposition of scenes widely removed in time or space? And how does he keep the narrative drive at such a high pitch when we know at the very beginning of the novel where Skipper ends?

In particular, Hawkes' use of detail needs consideration. Why these heaped up details? Why this economy? Why this pacing? Consider these two paragraphs, the first seemingly overblown, the second, hard and spare. On the bus:

> He had diced celery into cubes, had cut olives into tiny green half-moons, had used pimento. Even red pimento. The moonlight came through the window in a steady thin slipstream and in it Cassandra's face was a small luminous profile on a silver coin, the coin unearthed happily from an old ruin and the expressionless, fixed, the wasted impression of

some little long-forgotten queen. I looked at her, as large as I was I wriggled, settled myself still deeper into the journey—oh, the luxury of going limp!—and allowed my broad white knees to fall apart, to droop in their infinite sag, allowed my right arm, the arm that was flung across sleeping Pixie, to grow numb. I was an old child of the moon and lay sprawled on the night, musing and half-exposed in the suspended and public posture of all those night travelers who are without beds, those who sleep on public benches or curl into the corners of out-of-date railway coaches, all those who dream their uncovered dreams and try to sleep on their hands. Suspended. Awake and prone in my seat next to the window, all my body fat, still, spread solid in the curvature of my Greyhound seat. And yet in my back, elbows, neck, calves, buttocks, I felt the very motion of our adventure, the tremors of our cross-country speed. And I felt my hunger, the stomach hunger of the traveling child. (p. 29)

Then, later, at the high school dance:

"If the power fails," and I startled at the sound of Red's deep voice, glanced at the uncertain yellow glow of the caged lights, glanced at the windows filled with wind and snow, "if it fails there's no telling what all these kids will do. Might have quite a time in the dark. With these kids." And the two of them, widow in black, Captain Red in black double-breasted suit, swung out to the middle of the floor, towered above that handful of undernourished high school girls and retarded boys. Two tall black figures locked length to length, two faces convulsed in passion, one as long and white and bony as a white mare's face, the other crimson, leathery, serrated like the bald head to which it belonged, and the young boys and girls making way for them, scattering in the path of their slow motion smoke, staring up at them in envy, fear, shocked surprise. From the side lines and licking my fingers, swallowing the cake, I too watched them in shocked surprise, stuffed a crumpled paper napkin into my hip pocket. Because they were both so big, so black, so oblivious. But if this was the father, what of the ruthless son? What of Cassandra? What dance could they possibly be dancing? (pp. 80-81)

In both of these paragraphs the physical is firmly seen, grasped, smelled, tasted, and heard. Most important, however, Skipper (Hawkes?) is constantly looking around, checking on, remembering, suggesting, the various reactions to the things, to the elemental sensory facts. All characters are presumed as alert and aware and therefore by their very consciousness, responsible.

They also suggest the physical world as living, perhaps controlling, as evidenced by the black northern island and the multi-colored southern one. Furthermore, the protagonists in Hawkes' novels often have difficulty with the apparently static physical world. They bump into things, stumble or get lost since spaces are too small or too large. Clothes don't fit or get dirty. Moving objects—buses, horses, or people—cause even more confusion. *Second*

Skin, reduced to "plot," could seem a series of demonic pratfalls played by Charlie Chaplin or Peter Sellers. Or Lawrence Olivier if one recalls *The Entertainer*—and *Last Year at Marienbad.* The world itself, as well as time, intrudes.

I am tempted by one other question, one which is unanswerable and lies outside the novel: What direction would Hawkes have taken had he not joined a university faculty? It is obvious that *The Lime Twig* and *Second Skin* are more accessible to most readers than the earlier works. Is this the natural direction of his mind and imagination or is it perhaps the result of his experience with explicating a more conservative literature—or for that matter, his experience with explication itself? I am not suggesting for a moment a compromise for an audience. But a modification within the facts of existence seems to take place for the contemporary writer who cannot, usually, live on his art alone. What are the directions—or the hazards—of twentieth-century patronage?

The most recent bibliography is by Jackson R. Bryer (*Critique,* VI, 2 [Fall, 1963], 89-94), which is most conveniently supplemented by the annual bibliography in *Publications of the Modern Language Association.* There are no extended studies or biographies of Hawkes, but one should note Webster Schott, *The New York Times Book Review* (May 29, 1966), for some biographical details and Richard Pearce, *Stages of the Clown* (Carbondale: Southern Illinois Press, 1970).

Contents

1. Contemporary ¹ Reviews

2. Observations by Hawkes

3. The Growth of *Second Skin*

4. Essays

1. Contemporary Reviews

Erik Wensberg

Review of *Second Skin*

Improbably, the year begins with a major novel, *Second Skin,* by John Hawkes, to be published by New Directions.

In five previous books, John Hawkes has done everything wrong by prevailing taste—no obsession with American Civilization or the especially modern temperament, with regional decline and fall, or with social or political oppression. He may touch these, but only by the way, as he moves quietly and further into reaches of experience for which we really have no names.

Second Skin is told by its comic hero, an incorrigibly sweet, aging Navy man whose life has been continuously affronted by horrors. The narrative wheels gently over the terrifying landscape of his biography—the father's early suicide; the mother's subsequent death; the uncanny, frigid hatred of the beautiful daughter whose marriage dissolves in desertion and homicide; the suicide of a slatternly wife; refuge on a bitter Atlantic coastal island among bestial locals; near-fatal mutiny at sea; the daughter's suicide. Through a hundred humiliations and tortures this kindly, beefy, embarrassed and unkillable pantaloon moves finally into a paradise on earth that has the echoing breadth of myth.

The odyssey of "Skipper" is a grand vision, with nothing "unreal" or "special" about it; it is informed by a moral sense of life uncommonly complete, and by a freezing accuracy of detail in the midst of passion. If Hawkes's characters are, many of them, the very hounds of hell, his superlative gift for realizing alien hearts and minds endows them with absolute life. The daughter Cassandra, her piteous little foreign bridegroom, the black, cherubic Sancho named Sonny—with a stroke each is cut free from all apparent control by author, hero, reader. It is just this sense of roiling life, separate, uncontrollable, authentic as an earth tremor, that raises that sense of danger we do not want to know. That the simpleton prevails with implacable well-intent is not moralism: his is the opposite that proves the evil in life. Skipper's eventual paradise, "this floating island" in the Pacific or Caribbean, is likewise no less real than the ends of Shakespeare's last, grave comedies.

Indeed, Shakespeare and myth recur in oblique allusions throughout the book: Skipper could be, variously, Jason, Prospero, Odysseus; the landlady Miranda, all ruined abundance and gaiety, is a raging Medea; heaven and hell are islands. But such allusion is the final depth of Hawkes's art, not our admission to it. We have no more gifted novelist than this one.

Reprinted from *Vogue,* January 1, 1964, p. 22, by permission of the author.

Susan Sontag

Review of *Second Skin*

John Hawkes is still a young writer by modern standards (he was born in Connecticut in 1925). For nearly two decades he has been writing beautiful books which, while enthusiastically acclaimed by a small circle of readers, have failed to gain for him the wider recognition he unquestionably deserves. There are already three novels: *The Beetle Leg, The Cannibal* and *The Lime Twig*; as well as three novellas: *Charivari, The Goose on the Grave* and *The Owl.* In his fourth novel, *Second Skin,* there is no compromising with those qualities which have made him one of the half dozen authors of first rank in America today, no attenuation of the special strengths and manners of his work. Yet, one hopes that this novel will do the trick, and secure his position among that small group of contemporary writers whom readers and critics neglect at their peril.

Second Skin is the *apologia pro vita sua,* obliquely narrated in the first person, of Skipper (also called Papa Cue Ball), a 59-year-old former naval officer, fat and bald, with an ineffectual, anxious and lovable disposition. Skipper, who describes himself as a "lover of my harmless and sanguine self," is taking stock of his life during the months in which he is waiting for the beautiful Negress, Catalina Kate, to give birth to a baby who may or may not be his own.

Like Hawkes's other novels, *Second Skin* is a relatively short book, with extreme compactness. But where his previous books have stressed horror, *Second Skin* is ebullient and joyous; it is, in short, about horror surmounted by lushness and love. The past is the locale of horror; there Skipper belonged to a family with an incredible talent for death; there took place the suicides of Skipper's father, his wife and his daughter, Cassandra, and the murder of his son-in-law, Fernandez.

The present is the scene of Dionysian mellowness; now, as Skipper reminisces about his past, he is ensconced on an unnamed tropical island in a large, new informal family with an equally extreme talent for life, whose principal members are the pregnant Catalina Kate and Sonny, his former mess boy, who is now his best friend and possibly (if Skipper is not), the father of Catalina Kate's baby. *Second Skin* is thus about two things simultaneously—a second life, and a first life seen through the perspective of the second. The book ends after the birth of Catalina Kate's baby amid beautiful harmonies of flesh and friendship.

Hawkes manages to talk about all this horror and joy without being either

Reprinted from *New York Times Book Review,* April 5, 1964, p. 5. ©1964 by The New York Times Company. Reprinted by permission.

abstract or poetic (in the sense in which this is a vice for the novelist). *Second Skin* is full of the most exact observation, of beautifullly realized though not chronologically ordered 'scenes.' Some that come immediately to mind show Skipper dancing in a squalid San Francisco bar with Cassandra; Skipper shepherding Cassandra, her daughter, Pixie, and Sonny through a long Greyhound bus ride; Skipper getting mauled in a wartime mutiny on his ship; Skipper discovering Cassandra's suicide in a Maine lighthouse; Skipper prying a thirty-pound iguana off Catalina Kate's bare back.

Hawkes is an exact, wonderfully visual writer. Yet, precisely, he does not rely on his story to be self-evident. One has only to compare his treatment, in *Second Skin,* of the theme of a man shedding an old life for a more joyous and sensuous one with Bernard Malamud's recent *A New Life* to see the difference. Malamud's novel is shallow because it contains no point of view larger or more interesting than the very ordinary hero's very ordinary personal psychology. Hawkes's novel is compelling because Skipper is not so much an ordinary man (a realistic character in a realistic novel) as a palpable vessel of viscera and juices, his life not so much a story as a frieze of fleshy details. Hawkes does not just report the facts of vigor and renewals; his style enacts them.

For it is always, in a Hawkes novel, the style. He is the master of an immensely artful, corrugated surface of language—a looped, virile, restless style that really *is* the story. One usually speaks of an author's style, of course. But it's not enough to praise or disparage style; one must note the role of style in a given work. In some writers—say, Dostoyevsky or Dreiser—style is fairly unimportant; to say, therefore, that Dostoyevsky or Dreiser were sloppy or indifferent stylists is to say little against their work, which proposes quite different merits. But in a writer like Hawkes (like two other, very different, very good American writers, Djuna Barnes and Edward Dahlberg) style is—virtually—all. In *Second Skin,* style is the living incarnated form of the author's intelligence; everything is poured into it. Therefore, to say Hawkes's style is beautiful is scarcely to speak of something accessory. It is to speak of the life and intention of his books.

What makes Hawkes's books, however fine, still small scale, less than great? For me, these novels, with their intricate and allusively narrated plots, somehow fail wholly to connect with their major themes. The plot—vis-à-vis the theme—seems overgrown; as exotic details proliferate, the effects tend to cancel each other out. Then there is that persistent trait of understating the emotion of a violent scene, and Hawkes's habit of dramatizing the periphery rather than the center of an event. Sometimes I long to see some plain masonry behind the creeping vines and tendrils. But these are reservations which it is no doubt ungrateful to raise at this moment. The important thing to say now is that Hawkes is an extraordinary and admirable writer, and that in *Second Skin* he has written a beautiful book which is a worthy successor to his previous work.

Stanley Kauffmann

Review of *Second Skin*

The first question a prospective novelist must deal with today is one that did not exist for his predecessors a hundred or even fifty years ago: What do I mean by a novel? Until Joyce, the writer had only to make some fairly simple structural choices: straight or epistolary narrative; one character's viewpoint or multiple viewpoints or author's viewpoint. There were few other technical or formal decisions. Everybody knew what a novel was, and the difference between one and another were the differences between Trollope and Mrs. Gaskell themselves, between James and Mrs. Wharton themselves, not in the novel form.

But look at the past year. It brought us, among others, Beckett's *How It Is,* Genet's *Our Lady of the Flowers,* Cheever's *The Wapshot Scandal,* Rawicz's *Blood from the Sky,* Sarraute's *The Golden Fruits.* All are novels, but—content quite apart—they have as little relation to one another in form and method as is possible in imaginative prose works that are all composed of sequent lines of type on sequent pages. In each case the author, besides organizing his subject matter, has had to define for himself what he meant by a novel. In some cases—Beckett, for instance—any separation of form and content is hypothetical; the book could not have existed in any other form. Still Beckett had to make *that* decision. In other cases it is conceivable that the author might have used a quite different form. Among these authors there is little common ground; to each the novel is what he says it is.

This proliferation, which has analogies in the other arts, results from causes too complex to investigate here but which include such well-known factors as the enlargement of the middle class, Freudian investigation, religious and political and moral upheavals. Today proportionately more people can write, are more and more restricted to internal experience in straitening ways of life, and are increasingly aware that conventional literary processes are inadequate to their increased awareness of the subtleties of experience—or at least that

Reprinted from *The New Republic,* CL (June 6, 1964), 19, by permission of *The New Republic,* ©1964, Harrison-Blaine of New Jersey, Inc.

the subtleties that are accessible to conventional literature have now been plentifully explored.

John Hawkes, whose reputation is small but smoldering under the haystack of potential large acclaim, is another novelist who makes his own definitions as he goes. "Surrealist" is the descriptive adjective that has probably been most frequently used about him, and those who admire his work have said it is like a dream that makes sense. His fifth book, *Second Skin,* can sustain those descriptions to some degree, except it must be made clear that, syntactically, his novel is composed of orderly sentences, not Beckett's psychic gasps or Burroughs' verbalized hallucinations. It tells, in its own free fashion, the story of the narrator, Skipper, who in the present time-plane of the book is a retired naval officer of fifty-nine, living on an unnamed tropical island with a black mistress. She is about to bear a child who is either begotten by him or by Sonny, a Negro and his former Navy mess-boy, who shares his life on this paradisical island. The book flickers back and forth through various time strata, from which we learn about the suicides of Skipper's father and wife and daughter, the murder of his Peruvian son-in-law, a mutiny on Skipper's ship during the war. Skipper's second life (skin) in this warm place is untroubled by mundane fuss or social convention, a life that is loving, sharing, but unforgetting. He reflects that the deaths in his past happened after the war ended:

> . . . all my casualties, so to speak, were only accidents that came when the wave of wrath was past. But how can I forget what lies out there in that distant part of my kingdom?

There are hints of *The Tempest*: the luxuriant island setting, a character named Miranda, another anmed Fernandez (suggesting Ferdinand), Skipper's reference to himself as "an old Ariel in sneakers." But these references do not cohere and possibly are included only because Hawkes saw no reason *not* to include them.

As even the brief excerpt above shows, realistic criteria of characterization and dialogue are inappropriate. There may be (let us concede) naval officers who think like Skipper; it is less likely that there have ever been any who behave and speak as he does. ("'Got him now, Miranda,' I shouted. 'Rapacious devil'!'") He does not speak any more like a naval officer than Prospero (whom he resembles more than Ariel) speaks like a Milanese duke, and probably for the same poetic reasons. The other characters wear the proper masks and have the proper accents where needed, but are no more realistically treated and less deeply.

The story, "like to a murdering-place in many places gives me superfluous death." The suicides and murder carry no demonic strain, no Faulknerian doom; there could be more or less or, conceivably, none. Skipper could have had other "casualties" against which to pose his present life. The structure seems akin to that of a nineteenth-century opera libretto, without architectural imperative, easily alterable, condensable, expansible, primarily a provider of occasions for arias, ensemble pieces, ballet.

The arias and so on that Hawkes supplies are not "big" in terms of sweep and surge. The mutiny, for example, seems to be taking place underwater in slow motion. To Hawkes the novel is a machine for turning experience into images, and he uses his dramatic moments as bases for constructs of supple, gorgeous prose. There is little sense of fate in Skipper's unhappy life; we feel instead that Hawkes simply wanted to write a series of highly subjective scenes about a man experiencing various deaths and remembering them in various contexts.

His reliance on his prose as such is certainly not misplaced. His figuration, selectivity, his ear and eye are extraordinarily fine and untiring. But one flaw in his method is that it spreads. He seemingly forgets when he is not in a "scene," and he gives almost everything the same rich treatment. Virtually every millimeter of the book's fabric goes under the microscope of his intensified vision. For instance, when Skipper and his daughter are traveling on a bus at night, she hands him a sandwich:

> She moved—my daughter, my museum piece—and hoisted the sack onto her lap and opened it, the brown paper stained with the mysterious dark oil stains of mayonnaise and tearing, disintegrating beneath her tiny white efficient fingers. Brisk fingers, mushy brown paper sack, food for the journey. She unwrapped a sandwich, for a moment posed with it—delicate woman, ghostly morsel of white bread and meat—then put it into my free hand which was outstretched and waiting. The bread was cold, moist, crushed thin with the imprint of dear Sonny's palm; the lettuce was a wrinkled leaf of soft green skin, the bits of pimiento were little gouts of jellied blood, the chicken was smooth, white, curved to the missing bone. I tasted it, sandwich smeared with moonlight, nibbled one wet edge— sweet art of the mess boy—then shoved the whole thing into my dry and smiling mouth and lay there chewing up Sonny's lifetime, swallowing, licking my fingers.

It is remarkable imagistic writing. It can be analyzed in terms of its internal rhythms, the intricacy of the recurrent and varied figures in that small place, the sense of wholeness of each phrase, each sentence, the cumulation of the whole passage. It might almost stand, typographically rearranged, as a poem. But in a novel, still enslaved as we no doubt are by conditioning of the past, we recognize the beauties at the same time that another lobe is thinking: "For God's sake, it's only a sandwich. Eat it, and let's move on." Thus this method tends to flatten the topography of the book. For all Hawkes' care to include peaks of climax, the long prairie of sandwiches, etc., is bathed in the same golden light as the peaks.

Another peril in his method is indicated by V. S. Pritchett's recent brisk comment on William Golding's new novel:

> The inside view inflates the novelist at the expense of his people. And seen from the inside as "thinkers" and so on, novelists are bores. The more distinguished the more boring. Novelists are not entitled to these personal gratifications. I do not believe that theories of "contemporary aliena-tion," the "human crisis," or "our loneliness," etc., justify him in disposing of character. It is, at any rate, nine-tenths of our destiny.

The parallels between Golding and Hawkes are inexact but existent. For "thinkers," read "feelers," for "human crisis," read "crisis in the novel." Hawkes is not, like the Englishman, a dramatist of philosophical views, but his work is equally internal, equally far (in Irving Howe's phrase) from "the reality of *other minds,* minds quite unlike his own." The boredom—exquisite boredom, perhaps, in this case—of the solipsist scrutinizing his nerve-ends is inevitable.

The novel resolves to a solo virtuoso performance with props of people and incidents. Thus Hawkes disappoints in some measure even the reader seasoned by the "new" novel, perhaps because this author's sensibilities raise expectations of insight, of emotional effect, instead of well-articulated autism. I dare not aspire to Pritchett's note of pronunciamento, but perhaps I may suggest that Hawkes' definition of the novel is ineluctably and stringently circumscribed. Whatever his subject matter in this book, Hawkes seems primarily concentrated on its rendering, rather than its realization in us. The medium becomes to a considerable degree the object. Thus, although *Second Skin* certainly has other aims, it *seems* to exist for the sake of its admittedly exceptional prose.

Review of *Second Skin*

"A waxen tableau, no doubt the product of a slight and romantic fancy." When John Hawkes put those words into the mouth of Skipper, the narrator of his new novel, it must have been with some sense that *Second Skin* would probably be similarly patronised, with the reviewers admiring an indisputable skill (waxen tableaux are hard to create) and yet puzzling at a romantic pointlessness. Not that the visionary memory which elicits from Skipper this flash of self-revulsion is in fact merely slight and romantic—it catches with a comic lyricism the child's memory (fantasy?) of his mother being driven away in a primitive car, the car "severe and tangled like a complicated golden insect," the mother "raising a soft white arm as if to wave." There is an idyllic frailty about this moment, which follows hard on the black absurdity of his father's shooting himself in the lavatory, and is immediately followed by an anecdote which takes up "waxen tableau" with a vengeance:

My mother, unable to bear the sound of the death-dealing shot—it must have lodged in her head like a shadow of the bullet that entered my father's—deafened herself one muggy night, desperately, painfully, by filling both lovely ears with the melted wax from one of our dining-room candles.

Yet when we think of all the horrors that are perpetrated in Mr. Hawkes's novels, as in all those modern "Gothic" novels which Leslie Fiedler so admires, we may be inclined to take that waxen tableau in a harsher sense. It was Shaw, contemptuous of all the *grand guignol* which he saw in Jacobean tragedy, who fixed John Webster as a "Tussaud Laureate." Do the murders, suicides, mutilations, perversions, in *Second Skin* add up to more than a Chamber of Horrors? What is in question is not Mr. Hawkes's talent or imagination—he can write with a precise intensity on a range of subjects and emotions. The account in *Second Skin* of what it feels like to be tattooed, the pages which describe the difficulty of removing an iguana that has clamped itself to someone's back—these evocations are certainly not less than *tours de force*. But as with the violent happenings of *The Duchess of Malfi*, we find it necessary to ask what saves such writing from mere sensationalism.

Part of the answer would be the sense of humour. Humour is no guarantee of moral *bona fides*, but it does change *Second Skin* into something very different from Jacobean tragedy. To laugh at Webster is to annihilate him (as amateur theatricals are always demonstrating), whereas the poised ostentation

Reprinted from *The New Statesman*, LXXI (March 11, 1966), 339-40, by permission of Statesman & Nation Publishing Co. Ltd.

9

of Mr. Hawkes's style both invites and then freezes our laughter. It is the same with the purple patches: they know they are purple, and they choose—not succumb to—the cadences of blank verse. The decadent romanticism is not self-indulgent but is *about* self-indulgence:

> I heard the firmness of the dreaming voice,
> The breath control of the determined heart,
> The whisper dying out for emphasis,
> Hoping to keep her feathery voice alive.
> The darkest hour at the end of the night watch,
> When sleep is only a bright immensity.
> 'But wasn't Cassandra still my teenage bomb?
> And wasn't this precisely what I loved?'

That, and much more, you can assemble from less than two pages of prose. The rhythms are luxuriantly enervated, but they are not inadvertent—Mr. Hawkes's subject here is the romantic, intense, but preposterous and precarious love between father and grown-up daughter, a relationship which is tinged with incest but perhaps not more so than is commonplace.

Is it an accident that the father-daughter relationship should be a recurring obsession of Dickens, and that it should be Dickens whose prose most notoriously falls into blank verse? Gabriel Pearson has a fine analysis of this phenomenon in *The Old Curiosity Shop* (a novel in which sentimentality, humour, romance, deformity, and terror create a world not unlike Mr. Hawkes's), and he shows that the blank verse is sometimes altogether apt: "The primitive quality of the feeling is breathtaking: yet there is a corresponding mythic strength which is appropriately rendered in metre."

Mythic, yes. And it was surely the main gap in Leslie Fiedler's brilliant study of *Love and Death in the American Novel* that he seemed concerned with only one sense of the word "mythic." He says practically nothing about classical mythology and its relevance to these Gothic horrors. Mr. Fiedler sometimes writes as if the American imagination had created its terror from nothing but its Gothic predecessors and its own guilt. "The importance in our literature of brother-sister incest and necrophilia," the "obsession with death, incest and homosexuality"—these are true things to remark, but what needs also to be remarked is the similarity of such Gothicism to the doings of classical mythology. A father behaves so cruelly that the mother gives her son a knife with which the father is castrated as he is about to make love to the mother. A man finds that he has been made to eat his own son, runs away in horror, and later rapes his own daughter. A man who loses a competition is flayed alive. A treacherous servant is forced to cut off his own flesh, cook it, and eat it. The violence and perversion of such classical stories provide an analogue for the American Gothic. The myths of Greece and Rome, too, can share in Mr. Fiedler's observation that "the great works of American fiction are notoriously at home in the children's section of the library."

It is precisely the child's trustingness—dreadfully, fatally, persisting even in the adult—which creates the hideous terror of Mr. Hawkes's earlier novel, *The Lime Twig,* a story of racehorses and gangsters which suffers from the inevitable comparison with *Brighton Rock* but which has at times a remarkable force. The woman strapped to the bed and tortured by a sadist cannot believe that this can happen to her. Surely being innocent must save you—but it doesn't, because there is no cosmic headmaster. If there were, he might resemble Saturn. It is the same with Mr. Hawkes's first novel, *The Cannibal,* a distorted picture of Germany after the war, an eerie landscape of real and unreal cruelties. "Throughout these winters Madame Snow could not believe that the worst would come." But sometimes the worst will come, and not to believe so is one of the marks of weakness and of woe. At intervals throughout *The Cannibal* we catch glimpses of the Duke stalking a boy. We expect rape, but we meet cannibalism.

Too much need not be made of the fact that the desperate daughter in *Second Skin* is named Cassandra. On his first page Mr. Hawkes offers us not only classical allusions but also one of those strange fantasies of sex-change which figure so prominently in the myths.

Had I been born my mother's daughter instead of son—and the thought is not so improbable, after all, and causes me neither pain, fear nor embarrassment when I give it my casual and interested contemplation—I would not have matured into a muscular and self-willed Clytemnestra but rather into a large and innocent Iphigenia betrayed on the beach. A large and slow-eyed and smiling Iphigenia, to be sure, even more full to the knife than that real girl struck down once on the actual shore. Yet I am convinced that in my case I should have been spared. All but sacrificed I should have lived, somehow, in my hapless way; to bleed but not to bleed to death would have been my fate, forgiving them all while attempting to wipe the smoking knife on the bottom of my thick yellow skirt.

A father, a daughter and a wife all of whom commit suicide, and a son-in-law cruelly murdered—the tale is told through dimly-lit flashbacks, and it is true that Skipper was in a way right to be "convinced that in my case I should have been spared." He is not one of nature's murderees, and yet Mr. Hawkes never allows us to forget that the conviction that in our case we shall somehow be spared is one of our most foolish assurances.

But the mock-heroic in the style is comic, even if not only so, and it shows that the mythical nature of the horror is related to the other attributes which save *Second Skin* from sensationalism: its humour and its fully-conscious poeticising. If we want a parallel from the past, it will not be Jacobean tragedy but the Elizabethan minor epic, where Ovid's tales of violence and perversion, the "heady riots, incests, rapes" of Marlowe, were made into something new, something that did not deny the cruelty but was determined to find a cool way of reducing cruelty's power to drive us mad. The ambition of Mr. Hawkes's writing is not the impure one of making us tolerate violence, but that of helping us to find violence endurable.

The counterpart in classical mythology is also relevant to one of the first and most acute analyses of American Gothic fiction, an essay which still has not received recognition as a critical classic. Writing in the *Edinburgh Review* in 1829, William Hazlitt used the Gothic novels of Charles Brockden Brown in order to point the contrast with English fiction. The superstitions of England both authenticated and mitigated the violence of her fiction, as Hazlitt pointed out half-mockingly: "Not a castle without the stain of blood upon its floor or winding steps: not a glen without its ambush or its feat of arms: not a lake without its Lady!" But the Gothic terrors of Charles Brockden Brown were exaggerated just because they were created from scratch:

> They are full (to disease) of imagination—but it is forced, violent, and shocking. This is to be expected, we apprehend, in attempts of this kind in a country like America, where there is, generally speaking, no *natural imagination*. The mind must be excited by overstraining, by pulleys and levers.

And because of the lack of a potent superstition in America, "the writer is obliged to make up by incessant rodomontade, and face-making."

Certainly the modern Gothic novelists have too often gone in for rodomontade and face-making. The success of so much of Mr. Hawkes's writing—the feeling that he is a caricaturist rather than a parodist—has to do with his ability to make classical mythology take the place of that shared superstition which Hazlitt rightly saw as responsible for the hectic rhetoric of terror. But the peace to which Skipper finally comes, after the brutalities of a naval mutiny and of a suicide in the motel, is that which goes with his work artificially-inseminating cows, and *Second Skin* also succeeds because of its ability to impart warmth and esteem to such work. It has its failures, most obviously a dissipating fragmentariness which prevents the whole novel from ever becoming more than the sum of its best parts. But the neglect of Hawkes in this country makes it more important to remark the successes of this fastidious and frightening novelist.

Peter Brooks

Review of *Second Skin*

Since 1949, John Hawkes has been producing uncompromisingly difficult and often extraordinarily beautiful fiction. Although his most recent novel, *Second Skin* (published in America in 1964) may have gained him some measure of the public attention he deserves, his writing remains radically idiosyncratic, original, and isolated. While one could, especially in reference to his early work, evoke the names of Kafka, Djuna Barnes, or Nathanael West, Hawkes does not show any important literary influences. Nor does he refer us, in the manner of Alain Robbe-Grillet or Michel Butor, for example, to a set of philosophical assumptions which demand a "new novel." While he shares the French novelists' impatience with the conventions that make the novel a popular and comfortable form—illusion of intimacy with the storyteller, involvement with the protagonist, exploration of a recognisable milieu—his experiments in distortion, dislocation, and fantasy seem determined more by a sense of the effect to be gained by a twisting of traditional narrative modes. His primary concerns are rhetorical and stylistic, in the largest sense; he seeks to rewrite the world in depth, to realize, through exploitation of the illogical, grotesque, and obsessive, the full range of a reader's potential reactions.

His first novel, *The Cannibal,* is a nightmare which, in effect and technique, reminds us most of the Surrealists. Yet, while Hawkes has never renounced the intransigent antirealism displayed in *The Cannibal,* one is forced, in talking about *Second Skin* and the novel that immediately preceded it, *The Lime Twig,* to use a term like "clarity" to describe their almost classical economy and harmony of form. "Clarity" is misleading if it suggests ease in approach or a conventionally novelistic lucidity about "human nature," but it correctly characterises the brilliance of representation that Hawkes has achieved. By the persistent creation of order, structure, and coherence within his hallucinated imaginings, in *Second Skin* and *The Lime Twig* he has answered the promise of *The Cannibal* and redeemed the sense of disappointment left by his intervening work.[1]

This achievement marks a conquest within his own system. In *The Cannibal,* one found an historico-apocalyptic surrealist vision of a brutalized race, nominally the story of a German town called Spitzen-on-the-Dein on a day in 1945 when the unregenerate local patriots carry out a plot to kill the enemy occupier—a lone American who patrols a third of the nation on his

Reprinted from *Encounter,* XXVI (June 1966), 68-72, by permission of the journal.
[1] *The Beetle Leg,* and the two short novels, *The Goose on the Grave* and *The Owl.* Only the last of these seems to me to give reward for its difficulties. Another, early, short novel, *Charivari,* was published in the anthology *New Directions: II.*

motorcycle–and reassert German sovereignty in an illegible proclamation. This diseased, decaying, cannibalistic town insistently evokes another Germany–that of 1914–where an aristocratic form of life reveals its inherent sexual destructiveness, where characters act out the assassination of Sarajevo in their private lives: the innner necessity of historical destruction is powerfully suggested, and the analogical, even allegorical dimension of the novel is vividly apprehended. But the narrative of human events, personal relationships, tends to become lost. Hawkes' imaginative energy is expended on somewhat static descriptions of peripheral gestures of which the narrative status is unclear. Near the end of the novel, for example, we come upon a three-page description of the midnight attempt by the Duke–"an orderly man, not given to passion"–to dismember a fox he has killed:

> . . . he began to dislike the slippery carcass. It took all his ingenuity to find, in the mess, the ears to take as trophy, to decide which were the parts with dietician's names and which to throw away. At one moment, concentrating his energies, he thought he was at the top of it, then found he was at the bottom, thought he had the heart in his hand, and the thing burst, evaporating from his fingers. He should have preferred to have his glasses, but they were at home–another mistake. It was necessary to struggle, first holding the pieces on his lap, then crouching above the pile, he had to pull, to poke, and he resented the dullness of the blade. . . .

This passage superbly evokes the historical savagery, frustration, and lack of control which have overtaken the inhabitants of Hawkes' world. But this world is known only in such momentary "shots," projected and distorted by an intense illumination, tending towards any overall narrative coherence. And while we have to a degree been accustomed by Joyce, Faulkner, and others, to such a refusal to focus on the essential, we are here further confounded by the lack of an identifiable narrative tone, any point of view, however partial, obtuse, or unreliable, that would tell us how we should "take" Duke and fox. Conventions are the reassuring fossils of narrative attitudes, and unconventionality makes the reader feel a need for the orientation provided by a strong point of view.

But if an author revives convention in a certain manner, he can force it to do the work of point of view. This is what Hawkes brilliantly accomplishes in *The Lime Twig*: all the unreal but comfortably familiar conventions of the "thriller" are made to organize and interpret his psychological vision. The claptrap of a sub-literary genre–gangs of thugs, rigged horseraces, violence, orgies, and murder–are given a real and terrifying existence as inescapable realisations of our unconscious desires. When Michael and Margaret Banks, a lower middle class London couple, are led into a plot to steal and race a horse for the "Golden Bowl," they enter a publicized but unreal and forbidden world—a transgression which leads with rigid inevitability to an accumulation of terrors. Margaret is gently, urgently beaten to death by the gangster Thick in a scene which she accepts as "something they couldn't even show in films"—a region unrevealed by conventional presentations of horror, and censored by the waking self. Michael undergoes an extraordinary night of orgy—realization of all the erotic fantasies that attracted him to the outlaw—where he passes from the teasing whore Sybilline to the incarnation of his coveted London neighbour, "a girl he had seen through windows in several dreams unremembered, unconfessed." The morning brings, as if with moral inevitability, the shooting of a young girl (another inhabitant of his dreams) and Michael's strange "atonement": throwing himself under the horses in the home stretch of the race, to die mangled by the magnificent sensual beasts he idolised.

At the end of *The Lime Twig*, the Scotland-Yard types made familiar by the cinema—trench coats and black Bentleys—arrive, investigate, and set off to uncover "the particulars of this crime": a return of the convention which serves to remind us that the reassuring world to which it refers has gone under in a dark rite of sexuality and destructiveness. While in recent years both Robbe-Grillet and Butor have used the form of the detective story to suggest the deceptive quality of reality, the way it disappoints our efforts to find an underlying plot, Hawkes manipulates his convention to suggest the deeper reality of our attraction to the criminally violent and repulsive. As in myth and folktale, the fulfilment of our most profound desires is an accursed thing, for our passions are ultimately destructive of the self.

Hawkes' horror and terror have no metaphysical dimension: they are built into the banal and the quotidian. Hence the setting of *The Lime Twig* is an England rather like that of "Sweeney Among the Nightingales"—a disorderly, greasy world peopled by drab and vaguely sinsister men in mocha brown—constantly on the verge of becoming a Joycean Nighttown, where the self's orgy creates Circean transformations. A decaying Turkish bath, with its befogging heat and wet—"no place here for undervests or socks, tie clasp or an address written out on paper"—naturally becomes the scene of elusive encounters, murder, escape. In a public lavatory, the shady figures we instinctively fear do, in fact, turn out to be thugs armed with explosives, looking for us. Hawkes no longer needs the surrealistic imagery of *The Cannibal*, for here a slight pressure upon the conventional will produce the terrible. Here, the tone of hallucination is neutral, controlled, matter-of-fact, as when two of the gangsters strip the Banks' flat:

> They took out the tools of the trade and in half an hour shredded the plant that the cat had soiled, broke the china quietly in a towel, stripped linen from the bed and all clothing out of the cupboards and drawers and closets, drank from the bottle found with the duster and pail. They cut

the stuffing in bulky sawdust layers away from the frames of the furniture, gutted the mattress.

The high bells were ringing and Sparrow and Thick were done sawing the wood of the furniture into handy lengths, in sheeted bundles had carried out to the van the wood and the pieces of lingerie and puffy debris of their work. Bare walls, bare floors, four empty rooms containing no scrap of paper, no figured piece of jewellery or elastic garment, no handwriting specimen by which the identity of the former occupants could be known: it was a good job, a real smashing; and at dusk, on a heath just twenty miles from Aldington, they stopped and dumped the contents of the van into a quagmire round which the frogs were croaking. The two men smoked cigarettes in the gloom and then drove on.

This precisely detailed realization of a basic fear—loss of identity, loss of the self—slowly takes shape in a quiet, controlled, even humorous prose. We submit to the nightmare without wanting to, without being able to summon the power to protest. Such a style, such representations created from a slight rewriting of immediately apprehended conventions, permit the narrative coherence that *The Cannibal* lacked. None of the earlier novel's visual presence has been sacrificed, but here the story develops with a feverish exactitude to its final horrifying release. *The Lime Twig* is a gothic tale, but it is also a stark and beautifully formed object. While it does not pretend to clear up all its peripheral difficulties, or to impose an external logic on its theme, it finally leaves us with a sense of overwhelming lucidity about our relations to others, and to ourselves, a monstrous clarity about our passions.

Second Skin is a denser and more opaque book because it depends on a point of view both unreliable and banal. Its mode is apologetic: Skipper, bald, ageing naval officer, fat, sweating paradigm of incompetence, writes the "naked history" of his life to prove that despite the series of "brutal acts" to which he has been subjected, he is a man of both "love and courage." His apology necessarily takes the form of a series of isolated acts, arrested moments—a narrative method appropriate to Hawkes' scenic imagination—which he must attempt to understand and explain. The structure of his tale—complex, illogical, and emotionally effective—is the product of his combined evasiveness and sincerity.

Skipper sees reality as a "plot," but one which can be defeated by the nauseating repetition of love, softness, and solicitude. To the reader, this love, undiscriminating, misdirected, and repellent, at first seems simply a flaccid and inadequate response to the sexuality and brutality which surround Skipper. His courage hence appears mostly a pose: when his daughter is being raped by three soldiers under a cactus in the desert (and, we suspect, rather enjoying it), he holds her hand and murmurs, "Courage." But at the centre of Hawkes' novel there is something more important than incompetence. There is, once again, nightmare, a sense of total helplessness, the frustrated inability to make gesture accord with intention. With compulsive rapidity, the brutal acts of the obsessive plot take us deeper and deeper into the past—through the mutiny led by Tremlow aboard the *U.S.S. Starfish* (why? to what end? Skipper's inability to comprehend Tremlow's malevolence leaves a void in the account: "There seemed to be a purpose in that struggle, but still it escaped me"), through the murder of his son-in-law in a brothel, to the original, most brutal act of all: his father's suicide while Skipper, then a fat, blubbering child, tried to persuade him to live by playing the cello outside the locked bathroom door. When this is followed by two other suicides (his wife's, and that of his daughter, Cassandra) we understand that Skipper's tale, his cloying affirmation of love and life, is a response to the sense that he is surrounded and inhabited by death, that he virtually is himself death, and that everything he touches, despite his good intentions, turns to dust and blood.

The transformation of this curse, this legendary touch of death, into a blessing, may be accomplished on a "gentle island" where he can nurture a society of protection and love around Cassandra and her daughter Pixie. But his chosen Arcadia (a jagged, barren island off the Maine coast) turns out to be inhabited by lustful widows, priapic fishermen, and imbecilic, foul-smelling adolescents, all of whom conspire to baffle Skipper and satisfy what we now know to be Cassandra's considerable desires—even to her death. This disastrous establishment marks the end of Skipper's baffled attempt to deal with the treacherous world of passions. His "victory" is achieved rather in a "land of spices," a floating island where, with the assistance of his loyal messboy Sonny and assorted native females (Big Bertha, Sister Josie, and the pregnant Catalina Kate) he performs the function of artificial inseminator of cows. The impregnation of Sweet Phyllis is a lush pastoral rite which sounds as his personal triumph over ineptitude, mismanaged passion, and death:

Late afternoon and only faint sounds of breathing, brief shifting activity in the shadows, and Sonny was embracing the smooth alerted head while Catalina Kate and Josie were posted on her starboard side, were rubbing and soothing and curving against her starboard side and Bertha, Big Bertha, was tending the port. And I was opposite from Sonny and knew just what to do, just how to do it—reaching gently into the blind looking glass with my eye on the blackbird on Sonny's cap—and at the very moment that the loaded pipette might have disappeared inside, might have slipped from sight forever, I leaned forward quickly and gave a little puff into the tube—it broke the spell, in a breath lodged Oscar firmly in the centre of the windless unsuspecting cave that would grow to his presence like a new world and void him, one day, onto the underground waters of the mysterious grove—and pulled back quickly, slapped her rump, tossed the flexible spent pipette in the direction of the catchel and grinned as the whole tree burst into the melodious racket of the dense tribe of blackbirds cheering for our accomplished cow.

This prose, so different from that of either *The Cannibal* or *The Lime Twig,* has a luminous warmth which confers upon the scene, ludicrous and vulgar as it may be, some of the beauty and mystery of creation. Artificial insemination, reconciling impotence with fecundity, is the appropriate response to helplessness: Skipper's messy bovine peace, his surrender to nudity, pregnancy, and warmth, assumes a certain weird validity as an answer to the world of brutal acts. When, at the end of the novel, on All Saints' Night, Sonny, Kate, and Skipper, with the newborn baby (whether Sonny's or Skipper's is unknown, and no one cares), visit the cemetery and decorate a grave to look like a birthday cake, the dead celebrate life and the living celebrate the dead. There is reconciliation—"yesterday the birth, last night the grave, this morning the baby in my arms"—and the extravagance of rape and suicide seems rather more unreal than Skipper's survival. Resistance to Tremlows ceases to matter. Helplessness is transformed into slimy beauty and organic peace.

While *Second Skin* lacks the stark and horrifying lucidity of *The Lime Twig,* it has—as the passage quoted suggests—its own clarity: a clarity of the senses, a clarity of emotional landscapes rendered in full sensuous dimension. Hawkes' success is a question of total style; his senses and his imagination are alive, and his control of language—the choice of word and of intonation, the rhythms and the colouring—is remarkable. The brilliance of the moment found in *The Cannibal* has been shaped into an overall vision which we accept as coherent and intelligent. Hawkes' mature clarity finally convinces us that his difficulties are not diversionary or merely fashionable; the reader's effort is rewarded by the discovery of new terrors and beauties.

2. Observations by Hawkes

John Hawkes

Notes on *The Wild Goose Chase*

In Rex Warner's novel *The Wild Goose Chase,* a fiction of unusual climate, there are two men—the hero, George, and his companion of lesser capabilities, Bob—who have traveled "far on bicycles." These two are trying to gain entrance to The City, the place beyond the horizon of our imagination, by way of an academy called The Convent, where they are expectantly awaited by the headmaster. Their road is barred, however, by a Captain of Police and his foreign patrol. Without a moment's pause, the Captain subjects the travelers to the special examination prescribed for all who seek entrance into the academy:

George looked at the piece of paper on which was written: Candidates are requested to write their answers legibly and in as few words as possible. Every question should be attempted.

OPTICS
   1. What is meant by "Optics"?
ZOOLOGY
   1. Name two, or at most three, animals.
ECONOMICS
   1. (Need not be attempted.)
PERSONAL
   1. What is your sex?
   2. Are you fair-haired, blue-eyed, Conservative, Communist, tinker, tailor, interested in the drama, a wearer of spectacles, aviator, a drunkard, religious, musical, able to ride a push-bicycle? (Cross out inappropriate words or phrases.)
IMBECILITY TEST
   1. What material goes into the construction of a wall built entirely of brick?
   2. A snail is walking up a post. In every half hour it advances 1 3/4 inches. How long will it take to reach the top?

"What's the game?" said George, when he had read the examination paper.

All those still seeking the high mysterious flights of the Wild Goose, or concerned with that place into which the creative arts have fled, or who find the examinations stiffer as they grow older, must also ask the fair question,

Reprinted from *The Massachusetts Review,* III (1962), 784-88, by permission of the author and journal. © 1962 The Massachusetts Review, Inc.

"What's the game!" Bob, for one, could not pass this test until the Captain allowed him to copy George's answers.

I think the poet is better equipped to respond *resonantly* to such a questionnaire than the prose writer; the poet, to my mind, comes more easily to the spirit of the human test. Poets, for instance, thinking of the snail, can write: "I shaped out of bread a little animal, a sort of mouse. Just as I was completing her third paw, why look, she began to run. . . . She fled away under cover of the night."[1] Or

> The eager note on my door said, "Call me,
> call when you get in! So I quickly threw
> a few tangerines into my overnight bag,
> straightened my eyelids and shoulders, and
>
> headed straight for the door. It was autumn
> by the time I got around the corner, oh all
> unwilling to be either pertinent or bemused, but
> the leaves were brighter than grass on the sidewalk![2]

To me the poem—the eager note on the door—is the experimental effort in a short form. And when the experiment is the youthful practice of old men, when it no longer arises merely from the genuine need of the young but becomes the zealous vision in the older and brightly roving eye, then the effort is a firm, scandalous, and exciting thing. These are the poets who have no other purpose than to presume upon the peculiar unorthodoxy of their authorship; they sing the game. But there are also fiction writers who sing, who have private purposes, who hope for more in the novel than trying to build brick walls of brick.

Between poetry and the "longer form" of experimental fiction there exists a kinship, a seedling intemperate spirit, within which may be found the climate of the imaginative process. The climate is cold; the process is arbitrary, single-minded, a formalizing of our deepest urgencies. Like the poet, the experimental fiction writer is prompted to his narrative only by the vision which exclaims above him, or is driven to it from below; like the poet he enters his created world—loosening the shivers of his energy or restraining them—with something more than confidence and something less than concern over the presence of worms in the mouth. Like the poem, the experimental fiction is an exclamation of psychic materials which come to the writer all readily distorted, prefigured in that nightly inner schism between the rational and the absurd. And the relationship between the sprightly destructive poem and the experimental novel is not an alliance but merely the sharing of a

---

[1]Henri Michaux, "Enigmas," *Selected Writings,* translated by Richard Ellman (New York, 1951).
[2]Frank O'Hara, "Poem," *New World Writing:* 1 (New York, 1952).

birthmark: they come from the same place and are equally disfigured at the start. A comic sense of the dream, the presumption of a newly envisioned world, absolute fastness, firmness, insistence upon the creation of that other landscape where the moon hangs like a sac loaded with water or the devil wears "a lavendar shirt and thin black suit and a panama hat"[3]—this unchallengeable elevation of impulse and sudden poetic outspokenness drifts also through the climate of what we may still think of as "avant-garde" prose. As in Djuna Barnes' short novel *Nightwood*:

> . . . every movement will reduce to an image of a forgotten experience; a mirage of an eternal wedding cast on the racial memory; as insupportable a joy as would be the vision of an eland coming down an aisle of trees, chapleted with orange blossoms and bridal veil, a hoof raised in the economy of fear, stepping in the trepidation of flesh that will become myth; as the unicorn is neither man nor beast deprived, but human hunger pressing its breast to its prey. Such a woman is the infected carrier of the past. . . .

Recently *Time* magazine, pernicious as ever, dismissed the *Selected Writings* of Djuna Barnes by saying that the best of her work, *Nightwood*, offered little more than "the mysterioso effect that hides no mystery," and even Leslie Fiedler has described Djuna Barnes' vision of evil as effete. Yet all her myth and fear are mightily to be envied. Surely there is unpardonable distinction in this kind of writing, a certain incorrigible assumption of a prophetic role in reverse, when the most baffling of unsympathetic attitudes is turned upon the grudges, guilts, and renunciations harbored in the tangled seepage of our earliest recollections and originations. It is like quarreling at the moment of temptation. Or it is like working a few tangerines on a speedily driven lathe. Djuna Barnes is one of the "old poets," and there is no denying the certain balance of this "infected carrier" upon the high wire of the present. She has moved; she has gone out on a limb of light and indefinite sexuality and there remains unshakeable. She has free-wheeled the push bicycle into the cool air.

Djuna Barnes, Flannery O'Connor, Nathanael West—at least these three disparate American writers may be said to come together in that rare climate of pure and immoral *creation*—are very nearly alone in their uses of wit, their comic treatments of violence and their extreme detachment. If the true purpose of the novel is to assume a significant shape and to objectify the terrifying similarity between the unconscious desires of the solitary man and the disruptive needs of the visible world, then the satiric writer, running maliciously at the head of the mob and creating the shape of his meaningful psychic paradox as he goes, will serve best the novel's purpose. Love, for Djuna Barnes, is a heart twitching on a plate like the "lopped leg of a frog"; for Flannery O'Connor it is a thirty-year-old idiot girl riding in an old car and tearing the artificial cherries from her hat and throwing them out the

---

[3]Flannery O'Connor, *The Violent Bear It Away* (New York, 1960).

window; for Nathanael West, love is a quail's feather dragged to earth by a heart-shaped drop of blood on its tip, or the sight of a young girl's buttocks looking like an inverted valentine. Each of these writers finds both wit and blackness in the pit, each claims a new and downward sweeping sight and pierces the pretension of the sweet spring of E. E. Cummings. Detachment, then, is at the center of the novelist's experiment, and detachment allows us our "answer to what our grandmothers were told love was, what it never came to be"; or detachment allows us, quoting again from *Nightwood*, to see that "When a long lie comes up, sometimes it is a beauty; when it drops into dissolution, into drugs and drink, into disease and death, it has a singular and terrible attraction." But mere malice is nothing in itself, of course, and the product of extreme fictive detachment is extreme fictive sympathy. The writer who maintains most successfully a consistent cold detachment toward physical violence (as West does, for instance, when he describes the plump quail being snipped apart with tin shears, or describes the dwarf Abe Kusich being beaten against a wall like a rabbit) is likely to generate the deepest novelistic sympathy of all, a sympathy which is a humbling before the terrible and a quickening in the presence of degradation.

I think that we *are* unwilling to be either pertinent or bemused. But I too believe in fiction—hard, ruthless, comic—and I myself believe very much in the sack of the past slung around our necks, in all the recurrent ancestral fears and abortive births we find in dreams as well as literature. The constructed vision, the excitement of the undersea life of the inner man, a language appropriate to the delicate malicious knowledge of us all as poor, forked, corruptible, the feeling of pleasure and pain that comes when something pure and contemptible lodges in the imagination—I believe in the "singular and terrible attraction" of all this.

For me the writer should always serve as his own angleworm—and the sharper the barb with which he fishes himself out of the blackness, the better.

John Hawkes: An Interview

For many critics, your books show, if not the direct influence of, then affinities with, European works—perhaps more so than do most American novels. This connection may be a tie to a kind of internationalism noticed in the 'twenties, 'thirties, and 'forties, but less common now. Do you think American writers can learn anything from European writers, or is that period over?

An excerpt from *Wisconsin Studies in Contemporary Literature*, VI (1965), 141-55, reprinted by permission of the author and journal. © 1965 by the Regents of the University of Wisconsin.

Your word "affinities" seems to me more to the point than "influences." Certainly it's true that in many ways my own fiction appears to be more European than American. But the fact is that I've never been influenced by European writing. The similarities between my work and European work— those qualities I may have in common with, say, Kafka, and Robbe-Grillet and Günter Grass—come about purely because of some kind of imaginative underworld that must be shared by Americans and Europeans alike. I don't think writers actually learn from each other. But obviously we tend to appreciate in European writers what we sometimes fail to recognize in our own writers—that absolute need to create from the imagination a totally new and necessary fictional landscape or visionary world.

You mentioned Celine earlier this morning.

Yes, Celine is an extraordinary writer, and his *Journey to the End of the Night* is a great novel. His comic appetite for invented calamities suggests the same truth we find in the comic brutalities of the early Spanish picaresque writers, which is where I locate the beginnings of the kind of fiction that interests me most.

Let's turn to the older writers in the United States. For example, James, Hemingway, Fitzgerald, or Faulkner. Do any of these writers seem particularly significant to you at the present time—do they seem more or less significant than they did in the past?

As a writer I'm concerned with innovation in the novel, and obviously I'm committed to nightmare, violence, meaningful distortion, to the whole panorama of dislocation and desolation in human experience. But as a man—as a reader and teacher—I think of myself as conventional. I remember that after Faulkner's death, which followed so closely on the death of Hemingway, there was a kind of journalistic polling of critics and reviewers in an effort to assess our position and re-assess our writers in terms of influence and reputation. I think that at the time there was a general inclination to unseat the accepted great contemporary writers in America, to relegate Faulkner, Hemingway, and Fitzgerald to history, and instead to acclaim, say, Norman Mailer and James Baldwin. And we've also seen at least one recent effort to debunk the achievement and pertinency of Henry James. I myself deplore these efforts and judgments. James gave us all the beauties, delicacies, psychic complications of a kind of bestial sensibility; Fitzgerald's handling of dream and nightmare seems to me full of rare light and novelistic skill; Faulkner produced a kind of soaring arc of language and always gave us the enormous pleasure of confronting the impossible at the very moment it was turning into the probable. I think of all these achievements as the constants of great fictional ability. I think these writers will always survive shifts in literary taste and changing conditions in the country, and will always in a sense remain unequaled. Incidentally, after my reading last night a man asked me if there was anything of Faulkner or Faulkner's influence in my work. He was thinking of the passage from *Second Skin,* and I answered that I didn't see much Faulkner in that book. But as a matter of fact, while I was reading from *The Lime Twig* last night, I became quite conscious again of echoes of a Faulknerian use of inner consciousness and expanded prose rhythms. The echoes are undeniable, I think—Faulkner is still the American writer I most admire—though at this point I ought to insist again that in general my work is my own, and that my language, attitudes and conceptions are unique.

Such a view, then, would link you to the experimental writers of the avant-garde. As you know, the "avant-garde" was a rather popular concept about twenty years ago, but seems to be less so now. Do you have any views on the writer as experimenter?

Of course I think of myself as an experimental writer. But it's unfortunate that the term "experimental" has been used so often by reviewers as a pejorative label intended to dismiss as eccentric or private or excessively difficult the work in question. My own fiction is not merely eccentric or private and is not nearly so difficult as it's been made out to be. I should think that every writer, no matter what kind of fiction writer he may be or may aspire to be, writes in order to create the future. Every fiction of any value has about it something new. At any rate, the function of the true innovator or specifically experimental writer is to keep prose alive and constantly to test in the sharpest way possible the range of our human sympathies and constantly to destroy mere surface morality. What else were we trying to get at?

The concept of the avant-garde.

America has never had what we think of as the avant-garde. Gertrude Stein, Djuna Barnes, whose novel *Nightwood* I admire enormously, Henry Miller— no doubt these are experimental writers. But I don't think we've ever had in this country anything like the literary community of the French Surrealists or the present day French anti-novelists. And I'm not sure such a community would be desirable. On the other hand, in the past few years we've probably heard more than ever before about an existing avant-garde in America—we've witnessed the initial community of Beat writers, we're witnessing now what we might call the secondary community of Beat writers, recently many of us have defended *The Tropic of Cancer.* But I confess I find no danger, no true sense of threat, no possibility of sharp artistic upheaval in this essentially topical and jargonistic rebellion. Henry Miller's view of experience is better than most, Edward Dahlberg is a remarkably gifted writer who has still not received full recognition, I for one appreciate Norman Mailer's pugilistic stance. But none of this has much to do with the novel, and so far Beat activity in general seems to me to have resulted in sentimentality or dead language. My own concept of "avant-garde" has to do with something constant which we find running through prose fiction from Quevedo, the Spanish picaresque writer, and Thomas Nashe at the beginnings of the English novel, down through Lautréamont, Celine, Nathanael West, Flannery O'Connor, James Purdy, Joseph Heller, myself. This constant is a quality of coldness, detachment, ruthless determination to face up to the enormities of ugliness and potential failure within ourselves and in the world around us, and to bring to this exposure a savage or saving comic spirit and the saving beauties of language. The need is to maintain the truth of the fractured picture; to expose, ridicule, attack, but always to create and to throw into new light our potential for violence and absurdity as well as for graceful action. I don't like soft, loose prose or fiction which tries to cope too directly with life itself or is based indulgently on personal experience. On the other hand, we ought to respect resistance to commonplace authority wherever we find it, and this attitude at least is evident in the Beat world. But I suppose I regret so much attention being spent on the essentially flatulent products of a popular cult. A writer who truly and greatly sustains us is Nabokov.

I think many Beat writers have a kind of popularity. Whom do you think of as your audience, and what sort are you looking for?

The question of audience makes me uncomfortable. I write out of isolation, and struggle only with the problems of the work itself. I've never been able to look for an audience. And yet after a number of years spent in relative obscurity, I'm pleased that my books are gaining readers. I think that works of the imagination are particularly important now to younger readers, and I think it's clear that my fiction is being studied in colleges and universities. Apparently it's being read even by New York high school students. But at any rate I care about reaching all readers who are interested in the necessity and limitless possibilities of prose fiction, and I think there must be a good many of them. I'm trying to write about large issues of human torments and aspirations, and I'm convinced that considerable numbers of people in this country must have imaginative needs quite similar to mine.

One kind of reader is the critic. At its best, do you find any particular kind of criticism helpful—criticism appearing in larger circulation magazines or in smaller magazines? Does criticism mean anything at all to you as a writer?

I think the critic's function is mainly in terms of the reader. The critic makes the work more accessible, meaningful, and hence essential to the reader. I happen not to share the contempt for literary or academic criticism which appears to be current now. The critical efforts of the magazine *Critique,* for instance, which devoted one of its special issues to John Barth's novels and mine, are enormously helpful and gratifying. Generally I think I've benefited from criticism, though over the years what I've gained specifically from the critical judgment of a friend like Albert Guerard is almost too great to mention. I won't pretend not to be affected by newspaper reviews—in this area I'm easily outraged and just as easily pleased—but despite some of the silences and some of the more imperceptive or hostile responses, I have the impression that reviewers and readers alike in America are becoming increasingly receptive to original work. Certainly I've fared far better in America than in England where in one of the few sympathetic notices of my work to appear in that country I was described as a "deadly hawk moth."

. . . .

An aspect of your work that I have always appreciated, which I think many other critics have not, is the comic element. You have referred several times to comic writing—would you like to say something more about what you regard as the importance of comedy in your work?

I'm grateful to you for viewing my fiction as comic. Men like Guerard have written about the wit and black humor in my novels, but I think you're right that reviewers in general have concentrated on the grotesque and nightmarish qualities of my work, have made me out to be a somber writer dealing only with pain, perversion, and despair. Comedy puts all this into a very different perspective, I think. Of course I don't mean to apologize for the disturbing nature of my fiction by calling it comic, and certainly don't mean to minimize the terror with which this writing confronts the reader—my aim has always been the opposite, never to let the reader (or myself) off the hook, so to speak, never to let him think that the picture is any less black than it is or that there is any easy way out of the nightmare of human existence. But though I'd be the first to admit to sadistic impulses in the creative process, I must say that my writing is not mere indulgence in violence or derangement, is hardly intended simply to shock. As I say, comedy, which is often closely related to poetic uses of language, is what makes the difference for me. I think that the comic method functions in several ways; on the one hand it serves to create sympathy, compassion, and on the other it's a means for judging human failings as severely as possible; it's a way of exposing evil (one of the pure words I mean to preserve) and of persuading the reader that even he may not be exempt from evil; and of course comic distortion tells us that anything is possible and hence expands the limits of our imaginations. Comic vision always suggests futurity, I think, always suggests a certain hope in the limitless energies of life itself. In *Second Skin* I tried consciously to write a novel that couldn't be mistaken for anything but a comic novel. I wanted to expose clearly what I thought was central to my fictional efforts but had been generally overlooked in *The Cannibal, The Lime Twig, The Bettle Leg.* Obviously Faulkner was one of the greatest of all comic writers—Nabokov is a living example of comic genius.

. . . .

There are some personal questions here about how you write and you may answer them or not as you like. The first is, do you outline your novels before you start writing?

I've never outlined a novel before starting to write it—at the outset I've never been aware of the story I was trying to handle except in the most general terms. The beginnings of my novels have always been mere flickerings in the imagination, though in each case the flickerings have been generated, clearly enough, by a kind of emotional ferment that had been in process for some time. I began *The Cannibal* after reading a brief notice in *Time* magazine about an actual cannibal discovered in Bremen, Germany (where I had been, coincidentally, during the war); I started *The Lime Twig* when I read a newspaper account of legalized gambling in England. My other novels were begun similarly with mere germs of ideas, and not with substantial narrative materials or even with particular characters. In each case what appealed to me was a landscape or world, and in each case I began with something immediately and intensely visual—a room, a few figures, an object, something prompted by the initial idea and then literally seen, like the visual images that come to us just before sleep. However, here I ought to stress that my fiction has nothing to do with automatic writing. Despite these vague originations and the dream-like quality of some of these envisioned worlds, my own writing process involves a constant effort to shape and control my materials as well as an effort to liberate fictional energy. *The Beetle Leg* and *The Lime Twig*, for instance, underwent extensive revision. I spent four years revising *The Lime Twig* which, as you know, is a short book. And I must say that once a first draft is finished I certainly do resort to outlines, sometimes to elaborate charts and diagrams. But since I'm compelled to work with poetic impulses there seems to be no alternative.

Would you say something about your working conditions?

Like most people, I've written under a variety of conditions. I wrote my first novel in a writing class when I returned to college after the war; I wrote a short novel in the cab of a pick-up truck in Montana; I've written at night after work and in the early mornings before going to work; the first draft of *The Lime Twig* was written during my first academic summer after I began teaching; *Second Skin* was written last year on a kind of paradise island in the West Indies. In his book *Enemies of Promise,* Cyril Connolly said that one of the greatest obstacles to the young writer was the "perambulator in the hall." But I was married at a fairly early age and have always felt that the conditions of ordinary life, no matter how difficult they might prove to be, were the most desirable conditions for writing. My prose might be radical, but my habits are quite ordinary. On the other hand, I admit that I did have mixed feelings when a Guggenheim fellowship and several grants allowed me to take a year off from teaching at Brown—it was difficult to face the prospect of a year of ideal writing conditions without a certain amount of anxiety, especially since I had always resisted the notion of making special allowances for writers. However, I confess that now after those arcadian months in the West Indies—I worked on *Second Skin* every morning and spent the afternoon in the water washing away the filth of creative effort—I feel very differently about complete freedom and ideal writing conditions. *Second Skin* couldn't have taken the form it did without the time and locale made possible by the grants. I'm reminded that a few years ago Irving Howe gave a lecture at Brown in which he said that if Raskolnikhov tried to commit his murder today he'd receive a special delivery letter announcing that he'd been awarded a Guggenheim fellowship. It's an amusing and accurate comment on our own special artistic state of affairs and the risks existing today for the subsidized artist and subsidized culture. Subsidy seems absurdly contrary to the integrity of the writer's necessary anti-social stance. My own grants were unexpected boons which I look back on with nothing but considerable gratitude. I think that writers—and especially younger writers—should receive as much help and encouragement as possible.

To a certain extent you anticipated a few moments ago my next question, but I'll ask it, anyhow. To what degree are you worried about structure in your novels? Do you generally think of your novels in terms of a formal structure of the narrator, or do you discover structure as you write?

My novels are not highly plotted, but certainly they're elaborately structured. I began to write fiction on the assumption that the true enemies of the novel were plot, character, setting, and theme, and having once abandoned these familiar ways of thinking about fiction, totality of vision or structure was really all that remained. And structure—verbal and psychological coherence—is still my largest concern as a writer. Related or corresponding event, recurring image and recurring action, these constitute the essential substance or meaningful density of my writing. However, as I suggested before, this kind of structure can't be planned in advance but can only be discovered in the writing process itself. The success of the effort depends on the degree and quality of consciousness that can be brought to bear on fully liberated materials of the unconscious. I'm trying to hold in balance poetic and novelistic methods in order to make the novel a more valid and pleasurable experience. Of course it's obvious that from *The Cannibal* to *Second Skin* I've moved from nearly pure vision to a kind of work that appears to resemble much more closely the conventional novel. In a sense there was no other direction to take, but in part this shift came about, I think, from an increasing need to parody the conventional novel. As far as the first-person narrator goes, I've worked my way slowly toward that method by a series of semi-conscious impulses and sheer accidents. *The Cannibal* was written in the third person, but in revision I found myself (perversely or not) wishing to project myself into the fiction and to become identified with its most criminal and, in a conventional sense, least sympathetic spokesman, the neo-Nazi leader of the hallucinated uprising. I simply went through the manuscript and changed the pronouns from third to first person, so that the neo-Nazi Zizendorf became the teller of those absurd and violent events. The result was interesting, I think, not because *The Cannibal* became a genuine example of first-person fiction, but because its "narrator" naturally possessed an unusual omniscience, while the authorial consciousness was given specific definition, definition in terms of humor and "black" intelligence. When I finished *The Beetle Leg* (a third-person novel), I added a prologue spoken in the first person by a rather foolish and sadistic sheriff, and this was my first effort to render an actual human voice. Similarly, Hencher's first-person prologue in *The Lime Twig* (also a third-person novel) was an afterthought, but his was a fully created voice that dramatized a charcter conceived in a certain depth. This prologue led me directly to *Second Skin* which, as you know, is narrated throughout in the first person by Skipper who, as I say, had his basis in Hencher.

. . . .

I don't know quite how to phrase this, but it seems that in your work one of the things that is unique, in comparison with other modern writers, is the setting of your novels in an alien situation, one which you personally have never experienced as far as the actual milieu is concerned. You have never been in England, for instance, and the setting of "The Beetle Leg" and the others is far from literal. Is there any particular reason for this? Do you feel you are getting at important matters more effectively than you would have out of your own, more immediate world?

I take literally rather than figuratively the cliché about breaking new ground. Or I take literally the idea that the imagination should always uncover new worlds for us—hence my "mythic" England, Germany, Italy, American west, tropical island, and so on. I want to write about worlds that are fresh to me. But in his preface to *The Secret Agent,* Conrad speaks of the sights and sounds of London crowding in on him and inhibiting his imagination. And this danger of familiarity is something I've tried almost unthinkingly to avoid. As I've said, my writing depends on absolute detachment, and the unfamiliar or invented landscape provides an initial and helpful challenge. I don't want to write autobiographical fiction, though I admire Agee's *A Death in the Family* or the ways in which Conrad or Ford Madox Ford transform elements of personal experience and elements of subjective life into fiction. I want to try to create a world, not represent it. And of course I believe that the creation ought to be more significant than the representation.

John Graham

John Hawkes: On His Novels

GRAHAM: In *The Cannibal*, your first novel, then in *The Lime Twig*, a very exciting novel, all involved with evil, the chaos of human life, the frustrated false dreams, desires, you clearly are operating—and that is what makes you a somewhat difficult writer to read—you're dealing with time in a very curious way. Now with your enormous visual sense, and your ability to make real the present scenes in your novel, I'm struck by your ability to also make real the significance of the past which is *now* operating in the given scene. And also to make real some future, again, maybe some future desire or dream. Now, are you trying to say that the man—or the woman if she is feeding the cat—the man is taking a thread from his jacket or something like this, are you trying to say that this immediate act is some way, oh, I want to say "simultaneous" with all his past acts and all even of his future acts?

HAWKES: Well, that is a very nice idea. I think that's true. It isn't that I am trying to say simply that all life—that we're limited to the moment. I don't think I feel that. I suppose first of all I would be trying to get as much into the fiction as possible. And somehow I think we do have this sense that past, present and future are, in a sense, a kind of single whole. I am interested in your word, "immediacy," in having to do with fictional reality. I think that this is one very important aspect of fiction of the novel. In my last novel, *Second Skin*, that novel, though I think it was received on the whole very well—it has probably done better than any novel that I have written, and it's going to come out in the Signet edition of the New American Library—this to me is very fine and I am grateful for this kind of reception because I've worked long and hard and I haven't anticipated any, yet after fifteen years and as you move into the fortieth year of your life, you know, you begin to wonder a little bit. At any rate, *Second Skin*, though praised by many people, was also, in a sense, criticized for a possible looseness or piling up of detail

Reprinted from *The Massachusetts Review*, VII (1966), 449-61, by permission of the journal. ©1966 The Massachusetts Review, Inc.

and language itself and I think that that piling up of the thread on the coat—that kind of detail of an intense verbal, rhetorical, arcing kind of drive has to do with immediacy and I think that this is perhaps the primal level of fiction writing—the fiction writer's imagination, for me, exists primarily to beat inert reality into life. Now, in *Second Skin*, though I think that novel remains true to my own particular fictional or imaginative vision, I don't think I've really sacrificed anything, but frankly I have become increasingly interested in the conventions of the novel and in novelistic methods. Also, I have always thought that my fictions, no matter how diabolical, were comic. I wanted to be very comic—but they have not been treated as comedy. They have been called "black, obscene visions of the horror of life" and sometimes rejected as such, sometimes highly praised as such. In *Second Skin* I wanted to be sure, first, that the comedy would be unmistakable. Second, I wanted to use some of the fictional methods that I have become increasingly aware of—mainly the first-person narrator—so I used a first-person narrator who is a fifty-nine year old ex-naval Lieutenant, Junior Grade, a rather ineffectual man, who comes out of a world of suicide—his father committed suicide, his wife committed suicide. Finally the drama in the novel, the conflict in the novel, is the narrator's effort to prevent his daughter's suicide—he is not successful, she dies. However, he himself undergoes all kinds of tribulations and violations and by the end of the novel, I think we do have, in effect, a survivor. This is the first time, I think, in my fiction that there is something affirmative. In other words, even I got very much involved in the life-force versus death. The life and death in the novel go on as a kind of equal contest, until the very end, when a new-born baby, perhaps the narrator's, is taken to a cemetery on a tropical island, on an imaginary island, really, taken to a cemetery on All Saints' Eve with the candles lighted on the graves and so on. And out of this, I think, does come a sort of continuing life. The novel is about a bumbler, an absurd man, sometimes reprehensible, sometimes causing the difficulties, the dilemmas, he gets in—but ending with some kind of inner strength that allows him to live. And he lives, of course, with the memory of his daughter. He says he'll never forget what is out there in that other corner of the world—"Won't I always remember that" or something like that.

GRAHAM: It seems to me in your novels, *The Cannibal, The Lime Twig,* that you are dealing with the world of chaos, of falsification, of self-destruction, as you have, of course, with the suicides here in your last novel, *Second Skin.* Now, you use a word, about your protagonist in *Second Skin*: he does things which are "reprehensible," "causes" his own problems; also you use now the word "comedy"—the oh, I would say, sharp awareness that we have found in post-World War II writers of the closeness of comedy and tragedy. Why have we become so aware of that? Is it because we've seen such chaos that we can only keep it at a distance? Which would suggest, of course, that you can't "cause" things; almost, that there are no values or a great mixture of values. If I may interject a simple example, it seems to me that the sick joke, for let's say our grandparents, simply could not be taken in. Maybe even for our age, we . . .

HAWKES: Well, yes, I think there is still considerable resistance . . .

GRAHAM: . . . which suggests that we have some underlying values and principles that we might overtly reject, let's say, but which actually we are clinging to.

HAWKES: Of course, I myself actually, in real life terms or in art terms, I would tend to reject this sick joke, if it is merely a kind of dissolving into mindless and heartless obscenity or sadism. Cruelty.

GRAHAM: They're all sadistic as far as I've heard.

HAWKES: If it's merely that, I would certainly resist it highly. Now, on the other hand, Nathanael West, I think, did make use of a kind of sick joke, but I think he uses the sick joke always so that you feel behind it the idealism, the need for innocence and purity, truth, strength, and so on. This is at least implied. Now, it may be implied very faintly, or let's put it that the sick joke is saved by a kind of desperate joke, a larger desperate joke, that is in, say, West's work. Nathanael West, Joseph Heller, Flannery O'Connor. All of these are, I think, comic writers dealing in extreme violence. Bernard Malamud is, it seems to me, is—they call him—a magic realist; his humor, his comedy, is perhaps more obviously saving—I think that Malamud is a writer of extraordinary imaginative ability. I think his fiction is filled with something—I hesitate to use the word "grace" because it has special meaning or connotations—but his fiction lives out of a concern for humanity. I think all, I think any fiction that I would be interested in, would live out of that concern. Comedy works in two ways, say in my own work and in West, Flannery O'Connor, and in Heller, the comedy almost seems a self-inflicting affair, it is also a saving, a saving attitude. If something is pathetically humorous or grotesquely humorous, it seems to pull us back into the realm, not of mere conventional values but of the lasting values, the one or two really deep permanent human values. I think any writer of worth is concerned with these things.

3. The Growth of *Second Skin*

John Kuehl

Story into Novel

Mr. Hawkes "remembered that I had published a piece called *The Nearest Cemetery* in the *San Francisco Review Annual* (1963) and realized that this piece is actually the preliminary vision out of which my last novel *Second Skin* was generated."

. . . .

In the previously quoted letter of September 22, 1965, Mr. Hawkes also commented: " 'The Nearest Cemetery' is a compression of 20-30 handwritten pages prepared in the summer of 1960. *Second Skin* was written in 1962-63 and really could not have been written without the earlier microcosmic effort and the intervening two years of thought. . . . It seems to me there would be much to say about the various transformations evident between the original version and the book (the metamorphosis of the island barber as first-person narrator into Skipper as narrator, the transformations of various characters, the expansion of certain metaphors, ideas, etc., what has been retained and what omitted, the transformation of the plot itself—these all seem to the point)."

"The Nearest Cemetery" and *Second Skin* both employ first-person narration, but while the barber's story approximates the interior monologue, Skipper's resembles the dramatic monologue (with interspersed dialogue). The barber—totally unconscious of an audience—often moves forward associatively, as when the Princess' talk gives rise to a discussion of "the ear," which gives rise to certain things she said, which give rise to Mildred at the organ, which gives rise to the barber's impressionistic view of himself. Conversely, Skipper—highly conscious of an audience—organizes his main action spatially, beginning at "Chinatown" and ending at "our wandering island."

Although *Second Skin* does not borrow the associational method of "The Nearest Cemetery," it does borrow the earlier version's technique of juxtaposing past and present. In both, the present grows out of the past and is developed in considerable detail. However, the story's past—indefinite except for the day the marshal drove the barber to prison—has far less complexity and specificity than the novel's. The latter comprises several periods fitted neatly into an elaborate chronology.

That the tone of the two fictions strikes the reader as very different may be attributed partly to the dissimilarities between interior and dramatic

Reprinted from *Write and Rewrite* (New York: Meredith, 1967), pp. 265, 284-87, by permission of the author.

monologues. "The Nearest Cemetery" is a reverie, *Second Skin* an explanation; consequently, the interpretative problem of the first centers on what has been excluded while that of the second on what has been *included*. The author, who otherwise remains hidden, prefaces "The Nearest Cemetery" with a cast of characters, thus providing many particulars not contained among the barber's thoughts when we overhear them. But Mr. Hawkes, standing just behind and judging Skipper, provides irony to help us understand *Second Skin*. This establishes another and greater tonal difference between it and the earlier version which is straightforward.

Yet even after we have assimilated such information supplied by the cast of characters as "He loved her from afar and killed her," much must be inferred about "The Nearest Cemetery," whose vagueness typifies preliminary drafts. Did Mildred's obsession with the Lord and a deceased brother cause the barber to turn to the Princess? Was it a combination of his Puritanism and her promiscuity that motivated the murder? Why are the three actual lovers—Captain Red, Blud, and Jomo—also incarcerated?

The perplexities of *Second Skin* arise less from the material which has been omitted than from a misreading of the material which has been presented. If its narrator is taken at his word, he assumes the aspect of victim-hero surviving despite the world's malice. But this view completely ignores the author's bitter-comic irony: the discrepancies between what the character says and does. Skipper tell us that he is a courageous fellow, yet he always acts tardily and ineffectively. Skipper claims that Woman, in the person of the mannish Miranda who detests his *impotence,* is the archenemy, yet he drives both his wife (Gertrude) and daughter (Cassandra) to suicide. And while the bearer of the Good Conduct Medal considers himself to be the latter's paternal protector, his incestuous desires become subtly manifested through the vicarious pleasure he experiences when other men seduce her.

Perhaps the novel's most pervasive symbolism concerns death. Before committing suicide, the narrator's father was a mortician; afterward, Skipper—"one of those little black seeds of death"—suffers hallucinations over the demise of his mother and his wife during which he imagines a muffled chauffeur wearing goggles. There are numerous additional allusions to death, but the dominant metaphor is the cemetery.

This symbolic setting derives from the earlier version whose title would seem to refer to Bloody Clam Shell Island, the burial place of the barber's past. As with the mode of narration, the tone of the narrative, and the character of the narrator, it becomes more complex and specific in *Second Skin*. Skipper visits four cemeteries, each having sexual associations. At Gertrude's grave, he leaves his sword; at Cassandra's, the jar containing the fetus. At the high school dance, Bubbles, a "little girl guide" toward whom Skipper feels amorously attracted, leads him outside to a romantic rendezvous with Miranda, but when he approaches the cemetery—where children are buried and members of the senior class make love—he is pelted by snowballs. Finally, the book closes at the graveyard on the wandering island. Here Skipper and his followers celebrate the Night of All Saints.

To understand *Second Skin*'s death symbolism the reader must understand what has shaped the psyche of the narrator. The reason behind the barber's conduct remains shadowy; not so with Skipper's. At the very outset, he calls himself "the child-accomplice" in his father's suicide, and we learn later that the *action* he took to prevent "the shot" which "killed everything" may have hastened it. Victim of a traumatic experience, Skipper becomes an indirect victimizer. He forswears reality, refusing to examine inner or outer motives and refusing to *act* even upon things he cannot avoid knowing. Ego gives way to egotism, the man to the mask. As a result, Skipper never grows up, a circumstance made plain through his love life. He pursues little girls because he fears women, not realizing that sexual inadequacy, like impotence in general, is synonymous with sterility and death. At the end of the novel's action and the height of its irony, Skipper feels triumphant over death, but we know better. He may be a leader, yet his followers are illiterate Negroes. He may be a creator, yet only as an artificial inseminator on an island where steers try to impregnate cows and cows other cows. Skipper may be a master, yet the mistress is an adolescent female. Responding to the question, "Who do you think it looks like, Kate? Sonny or me?" she says of the baby, "Him look like the fella in the grave."

"The Nearest Cemetery" contributed several characters besides the narrator to *Second Skin*. Of these, its Princess is the most significant, for she inspired the novel's two principal women, Miranda and Cassandra. Like the first, whom Skipper thinks of as a princess, the Princess of the story wears slacks; like the second, she has a small child; and like both, this "unhappy wife," this "woman of beauty" flirts and sleeps with the barber's male acquaintances. That he loves her "from afar," then kills her reveals much about the later version since it is a conscious enactment of Skipper's unconscious attitude toward his daughter.

Captain Red, Jomo, and Blud are not related in "The Nearest Cemetery" but become members of a single family in *Second Skin*. No longer the barber's brother-in-law or the lighthouse keeper or the Princess' lover, Blud appears there as the boy Bub. Captain Red remains the bald, middle-aged master of the *Peter Poor,* while Jomo—who has acquired an artificial hand—continues to be characterized by his baseball cap and his "black hair plastered down with pine sap." Jomo's mother is displaced by Captain Red's mother and the barber's wife gives her name to Skipper's mother. Because "The Nearest Cemetery" influenced only "The Gentle Island" portions of the novel directly, the story does not have many of the novel's other important figures.

By the same token, however, Bloody Clam Shell Island served as model for the setting of these portions. Its church, lighthouse, clapboard house, gasoline pumps, orange pop, Crooked Finger Rock, and overturned rowboat are among the properties which *Second Skin* borrowed.

John Hawkes

The Nearest Cemetery

Scene of narration: a small state penitentiary in New England.

Characters:
   THE PRINCESS: summer visitor to Bloody Clam Shell Island; unhappy wife of a New York meat packer; woman of beauty; victim of the local barber.
   MILDRED: The barber's wife.
   CAPTAIN RED: lobsterman in his fiftieth year; first lover of the Princess.
   BLUD: lighthouse keeper; Mildred's brother; second lover of the Princess.
   JOMO: off-island gas station attendant and vicious small-town sport; third lover of the Princess.
   THE BARBER: narrator; fourth and final lover of the Princess. He loved her from afar and killed her.

I remember the day—blue, puffy white, orange—and that I was smiling until we passed a hot dog stand and a shingled church with windows as bright and painful as some of my own dreams. In the darkness my eyes began to heal. But the car was twisting over a torn-up section of the road or pushing between the pines or darkening the corner of a plowed field, and I couldn't smile. I remember the smell of upholstery and gasoline and vomit and the sound of the Marshal talking to himself the whole way. He looked like Vinny who wore a poppy in his cap. Suddenly I blinked and through the window I saw Blud's lighthouse standing in a plot of dry yellow sod, Blud's lighthouse by the side of the road and rising up from dead ground and sand instead of the bright wet rocks that always looked as if they had been freshly painted with black tar. But it was a hot dog stand. Another hot dog stand and closed for the season.

Reprinted from *San Francisco Review Annual*, I (1963), 178-85, by permission of the author and New Directions Publishing Corporation. Copyright © 1963 by John Hawkes.

We drove through Jomo City and there, in the door of the trailer, was Jomo's mother husking an early ear of corn. A heap of pop bottle caps was sparkling out of the tall grass at her feet, and Jomo's mother made me think of Mildred, except my Mildred lives in an unpainted clapboard house on Bloody Clam Shell Island instead of in Jomo City in a trailer with flat tires and propped on concrete blocks in the tall grass. The old woman did not look away and did not wave, though she recognized the car and shadow that fell within twenty feet of her and swallowed the three gasoline pumps—two were dry—and even though she knew I was the only passenger that day. But between the trailer and the pumps was an overturned rowboat with a hole ripped in the bottom and, before the dust settled and we passed once more into the damp pines, a small dog thrust his head and paws out of the hole in the rowboat and barked as he might at a great crow flying across the woman's head. There was sun in the dog's mouth, sun reflecting from the bottle caps and from the antennas Jomo had rigged on the trailer's roof.

The Princess always stopped in Jomo City to fuel her car. The old woman worked the pump while Jomo brought bottles of orange pop for the Princess and her little boy, Jomo whose brown arms bare to the shoulder were washed with gasoline and whose hair is still a wavy cap of pitch, Jomo who sometimes let the little boy shoot at the rowboat with an old .22 calibre rifle hung inside over the trailer door, or at a piece of window glass propped against a stump while the Princess leaned out of the white Cadillac and laughed and smelled the salt in the air. Princess always brought Jomo's mother a bottle of perfume from New York and next Saturday at three o'clock, when the old woman comes in with the rest, Jomo and Captain Red and Blud and I will smell the odor of that perfume again and think, each in turn, of culvert or open sea or the town hall or the Princess coming down the rocks like a little plume fluttering in the sun or the pinging of the rifle and the smash of glass (all of us will remember that the Princess had a mouth the color of the orange pop Jomo gave her in the cold wet bottles he wiped with his undershirt)—and all because of a few drops of scent daubed behind the ear of an old woman who sits heavily on her trailer steps in weeds and wears a corset, Jomo says, which she repaired with pieces of black inner tube.

Like an island. In the first sunset that prison was an island without rock or spume or salt, an island without buried barns and sea air pollinated and apples that fall from fractured boughs to rot on the shore line with the periwinkles—island almost the size of Bloody Clam but with gongs and siren instead of buoys and twenty-eight miles inland from the sea. So that day I only went from one island, Bloody Clam, to another island lying in a white valley across which move not boats, orange and black, but a few muddy dump trucks and, occasionally, the Marshal's car.

Each of us has his Venus—four men and four women who are either mothers or wives—Venus at least in memory. And if there is no seaspray here, no Crooked Finger Rock, there is at least the wind, though wind over watch towers and down lengths of walls makes other sounds, whether moan or sough or shriek, than it does through the worm-holes in unpainted clapboard or when it is bending the tops of pines that ring the burning town dump of a little island town. With the wind, on which I smell the blood of fish, and with masonry and with fixed perimeter that is nonetheless fluid rather than geometric, the walls buttressed against open fields, road and village in a circumference vaguely but not perfectly circular, the prison is in itself an island (and time is the calm, or time the hurricane) but further it brings to mind the lighthouse because of the white painted stone, the metal underfoot thick with coatings of gray heavily-leaded paint, lighthouse because of the narrow walks and odors of fresh paint and oil and half-inch sheets of glass blinding, at sunset, high above our heads and behind bars. Island of men; lighthouse large enough to contain so many men each with his own Venus (though in memory; though only some approximation of her who charmed, each to her liking. Blud and me and Jomo and the Captain) and each with denim pants and coat and face like that of the keeper and the kept combined, since in his tower at dusk the lighthouse keeper shows his enchantment in his white stubbled jaw and eye that looks and looks nowhere except down the three-mile path of his silent light toward a sea from which no ship may rise and approach because of the very nature of that eye's desire, the very nature of that light's dangerous beam. It is the lure that warns away the catch.

My shop is empty on Bloody Clam, empty and boarded up, and the hair will grow long on Bloody Clam Shell Island. But here I keep most of the heads of hair cut short, and every day I shave the allotted number of white jaws and cheeks the texture of a field of lice. Among so many men, week by week, I wait until it is their turn and they come to me; and I smile, knowing that first this neck and ear and hairless scalp—it is forever speckled red and white with sunburn and bears a scar—and this temple-pulse of the oldest man of them all belong to the captain of the *Peter Poor*. And next I find that I am lathering the swollen cheek of Blud, my own brother-in-law. (Isn't he like Mildred? Mildred to a tit?) Jomo still has his curls, the blue-green hair sticky with pine sap. Then one day I notice my hands are becoming sticky. And I turn the chair and my razor shapes those sideburns—they are the color of trees in gloom, the color of water at high tide—and I remember the black T-shirt with the sleeves cut off at the tight shoulder seams, and I remember the bleached purple baseball cap he wore high and tight and perfectly horizontal on the living hair. A faded baseball cap he wore for Princess. And I reach for the hot towel and on the end of my finger see the little red line as bright and delicate as something you might see wriggling in the eyepiece of a microscope. I stop for a minute and suck it clean. Then with the towel in my hand I see again that he has a chin, rounded to a point and firm and white as a duck's egg, and that he has a mouth unmistakable and two lips bowed and dry and faintly red and capable of moistening or smile. He has all this, the hair and chin and lip. He had them for Princess. Carefully I brush on the powder and sometimes, holding the talcum flask in one hand and, in the other, the silver shears—sometimes I wonder if all those features won't suddenly disappear when I wipe off the powder. There is no talking in this barber shop; I talk with none of them. But I know their heads, their hair, I know what they did. And each of them knows me. And our eyes meet in the glass.

They—these three—were waiting for me when I arrived. I knew that despite the identical denim pants and shirts and coats and despite these numbers of men, they would find me, or I them. I knew that they were waiting and, in shoe factory or corner of the yard or high on a catwalk, would be standing or walking slowly or gesturing together out of their common dream. And now I wait for them. There is no talking in the barber shop, or in the yard or factory; no talking here, except for a single half-hour after dinner at noon and yet during all the hours measured by the moving shadow of a tilting shotgun's barrel and on through the dark hours when the men lie on their backs asleep or smoking—during all this time the forbidden word goes around from tier to tier, from one end of our state's island to the other. Only a joke (about Johnnny in the privy, about the old white horse) or a plan to steal knives (I listen in such cases but never reply). But whatever word it is, it goes around among us like temper shooting down a row of quickening hands or the laugh that only we can see on faces expressionless and cold. Talking is against the rules and you have to be able to read the tongue still thrust into a cheek or hear the drag of the foot or the sound hissing from between two front teeth. No talking here. And yet for most of them, for me, there has been no talking all their lives (or mine). At least there is no talking on Bloody Clam Shell Island, very little requiring actual speech or anything more than the slow ceremonial of the dumb, the daily slow hustling of the island's dumb. But honor and piety or desire and stealth create different silences, and the child learns to hold out his cup, the waitress to set down the plate, a man his money. The child learns to get from the cemetery to the barber shop without a word, from the wild still competition and gainless amusement of the single bowling alley to the salt and blood and danger of the fish-bait bench without a word. The man has already learned his silences. Through habit. Through years of practice. Through contempt or love or inability or weeks and months of long days when the wind is too high to talk, the sea too rough.

The wordless life. The lifting of his chin for a fight, the tossing of his head for a kiss. And everything is in the lift of an eye, a hitching of the hips, the tossing of his head after a bottle of beer drunk under the herring boat docks in the mud at low tide or the way spring daisies appear wordlessly bound into a bun of hair. One sentence will sell boats, nets, house and land; one sentence will serve for a whole night and get a child. Nobody talks more than that. But everybody knows. Like Johnny in the privy or the white horse. There are six hundred and fifty people on Bloody Clam and three thousand convicts here. And none of them are talkers. They never were.

But the Princess talked. Each summer from the moment her yacht first came flashing into the green harbor and she stood on the bow in sunglasses and silk trousers cut like a man's and waved, with her little boy propped in a deck chair behind her and the husband buried away in the pilot house, until the day she left (always last to board the white boat with the crew and child and husband looking up at her and waiting to cast off) the Princess talked—talked all over the island—and on a clear day it would be the only voice to hear, the foreign tongue and fairy tale accent coming down from the hill in a lilting continuum we knew was words (so many she might have been reading aloud or singing aloud the pages of a book) and someone rolling a cigarette or someone holding a knife with a slimy and silvery hand would hear that voice and listen, not stopping the fingers or staying the hand, but listen and nod perhaps if there was anyone else nearby. But the Princess would be too far away for the old men to hear and they would go on looking at their feet or sleeping with their backs dusty and humped in the sun. Sleeping, not knowing what they missed.

I lie on my back just waiting to hear it all again, just listening. Because the ear is already packed with sound like the hollow tree or the dog's skull in the dump or the coffin Vinny carries out of town in his garbage truck. Every object—length of wood, weight of bone—and every place already contains its fill of sound and the ear is its own coffin, its own little reverberating casket that hears everything it was ever meant to hear at any moment of the night and even though sometimes you want to sleep and so lie there holding it beneath your trembling hand. Your ear. The barber's ear.

The ear is the coffin that can't be closed or nailed or buried—it is forever warped with so much sound—and through the snoring and scraping of the old men in the sun I hear the girlish floating of words founded in peculiar tingling accent (*Good morning, boys*) or among the picking of the rats in the dark Town Hall I hear it again (*Poor Blud, poor Blud*) and through the rumble of the captain pulling on his boots, fishing for the patched rubber, feeling about and then jamming in a foot like a cannonball puffing into a mountain of used car tires I hear it still clear and round and insistent at five o'clock in the morning (*Take me out on the water with you, Red*) and sometimes I can make out what she said to Jomo and sometimes I can't, and then (despite the singing of the larches and the rote of the sea and the wind and the clattering of Vinny's truck outside) she talks just to me.

So the mind lies between the echoing coffins of the ears—a barber's ears—and you try to calm it in the midst of all that roar and whisper while a shadow falls through the bars and sweeps your chest. But then I raise my hands; I hold one ear; I hold both of them; I press with my palms. Because then it is not Mildred's voice I hear—not the voice, though I hear it often enough—but rather Mildred playing steadily on the church organ, Mildred pumping her feet, Mildred pushing the keys and Mildred making the reeds and seagulls shriek. And in each of Mildred's chords is the heavy harmony of the Lord and bass voice of Mildred's other brother who died from drink. And I cannot bear to listen. The barber cannot bear to listen to Mildred pumping and marching with the Lord at the town's church organ. The Lord and Mildred deafen me. They make me think of lying dead and naked beside the body of the shipwrecked woman on Crooked Finger Rock at the height of the gale.

Short as the watch that ends the night is what I hear, and *Time, like an ever-rolling stream, Bears all its sons away* is what I hear, the phrases filling the mind with their monotony and fear, and *They fly, forgotten, as a dream Dies at the opening of day*—all of it this booming, this beating of hymn on slick shingles and empty beach, and the Lord and Mildred are bearing me away to the Rock. Singing. Bearing off the naked barber to the heart of the hymn that is the gate, carrying me away at the center, easily, while the plankton spurts aloft into the dark of the storm, and I fly, fly, while Vinny cranks his truck in the wind and Mildred sings with the lost brother.

The barber. But even the barber has his tongue and toes and fingers, his hidden hair. The barber too has his lungs of twisted and dampened paper, his ears in which the islands float, his eyes that gleam, his sensitivity to skin, to touch. And sometimes I think I am all water. Hair and water. What the crack leaps upon, leaping to deform the image further, is nothing and my shop is on Bloody Clam Shell Island—closed, safely boarded up—while I am here.

4. Essays

S. K. Oberbeck

John Hawkes: The Smile Slashed by a Razor

Astonishing sympathy, satanic humor, cold detachment: these playful postures best describe the experimental fiction of John Hawkes, who "finds both wit and blackness in the pit." Ten years ago, Hawkes still had what critics of faint praise and damnation called "a tense following." *The New Yorker,* taking note in 1949 of *The Cannibal,* observed that Hawkes "writes like no one else at all." Only slightly less daring, *The Saturday Review* dubbed the book "an extraordinary work of fiction." Another publication mumbled something about "troubling nightmares" and rolled over, one presumes, with a few grams of Seconal to try to forget about John Hawkes. But his writing leaves an indelible mark in the mind, a cloven hoofprint stamped in brass.

His later novels, *The Owl, The Goose on the Grave, The Beetle Leg,* and *The Lime Twig*—in addition to his first novella, "Charivari"—got passing notice of the same undernourished consistency from consumer news and literary magazines. For Hawkes has never been treated by popular publications to the largesse granted such authors as Salinger, Mailer, Bellow, Roth and Malamud. This is a pity since he writes with deeper talent and conviction than any of these.

Time seems neither to mellow nor sophisticate the average reader of experimental fiction; time does, however, mellow and sophisticate an author to a point where he can elbow his way (he has to, it seems) into the front ranks of the publicity patch. Bemused very slightly over his following, and quite unexcited over the lack of a nice, personal tidbit about him in *Esquire,* Hawkes has changed his prose very little and continues to maintain his basic impulse and energy. He has developed, as Albert Guerard predicted in 1949, a tendency toward the more realistic form of extended fiction. The development of his capacities, seen in passing from "Charivari" to his recent *Second Skin,* will astonish most of his readers.

Leslie Fiedler wrote an introduction to *The Lime Twig* as if he were discovering Hawkes to the common market, but he made many lucid comments about his reactions to the book. He saw the author as a rebel writing in an age of literary recapitulation, when traditional novels are rewritten in a number of inventive ways. Certainly it is true that Hawkes happens to be a rebel in the present spectrum of modern literature. It could

Reprinted from *Contemporary American Novelists,* edited by Harry T. Moore (Carbondale: Southern Illinois University Press, 1964), pp. 193-204. Copyright © 1964 by Southern Illinois University Press. Reprinted by permission of Southern Illinois University Press.

hardly be otherwise. And certainly it is gratifying to read his highly original and difficult prose in this period when too much of our fiction seems smoothly tailored for a specific market or audience. Perhaps it is much to his credit that Hawkes would seem out of place, really *too* disturbing, in *The New Yorker, Esquire, Playboy* or *Atlantic Monthly*—no matter how nearly acceptable his flamboyant grotesque and vision of terror.

While it is true that Hawkes writes like, sounds like, no one else at all, it is equally true that his fiction "shares a birthmark," as he puts it, with a body of writing that might arbitrarily be represented by authors such as Faulkner, Kafka, Conrad, Lautréamont, Djuna Barnes, Flannery O'Connor, Nathanael West and Kraft-Ebbing. His pure creative energy, mordant and mundane, has the effortless sting and bite of these authors and their names come readily to mind when one discusses Hawkes.

But to talk of his fiction merely by relating it to another body of writing is to dismiss his consistent and truly original talents. For, obviously, Hawkes tailors his fiction to no standard but his own, "the satiric writer, running maliciously at the head of the mob and creating the shape of his meaningful psychic paradox as he goes." He is unafraid to step out into the thin, cold air of what he calls "a climate of pure and immoral *creation*." His fictions are totally refined abstractions, clear enigmas poised in brilliant rhetoric, evoking the inexorable, unhurried and deliberate touch of terror.

The richness of his prose resists neat critical summation, for his is a disturbingly resonant and precise language, expression urged from an intense clash with our deepest obsessions and everywhere rewarded with what Guerard calls the author's "demonic sympathy." This sympathy, Guerard observes, enters "into the saved and the damned alike." All characters bask in its cruelty, all events are tinged by its love, for to understand everything is to ridicule everything—or to sympathize with everything. In this posture is a curious banality, and many of Hawkes' readers find it difficult to separate sympathy from ridicule in his fiction. They are much the same. When Thick beats Margaret Banks in *The Lime Twig,* one feels a quickening in the prose, a tensing of cadences, almost a rhetorical sense of jubilation. Here is something about which one can write! I thought of Flaubert as I read that deliciously horrible passage, how he dwelled with an almost similar delight on the slow death by poison of Emma Bovary. The excessive detail, clinical authenticity, long, lingering view, full of love and hate, at Emma expiring . . . Surely Flaubert enjoyed getting rid of Emma finally. He almost dances on her empty coffin, though he was said to remark, "Emma Bovary, c'est moi!" The novelist too must be able to satisfy his frustrations violently.

Hawkes also finds a mixture of pity and exhilaration in such violence, in the objective evidence of what he calls "the terrifying similarity between the unconscious desires of the solitary man and the disruptive needs of the visible world." Surely his pity for Margaret is tinged with pride in the fine job he was doing, through Thick, on her. In each of his novels, Hawkes grimly uncovers both the "unconscious desires" and the "disruptive needs," making them objective in a particularly creative way.

In both his conception and his language, one feels a tremendous compression, the sense of suffocation Flannery O'Connor said she experienced reading *The Lime Twig*. To borrow from Camus' *The Rebel*, one might say that Hawkes writes in such a way that "the malady experienced by a single man becomes the mass plague." When, again in *The Rebel*, Camus discusses Lautréamont, he remarks

> We find in Lautréamont this refusal to recognize rational consciousness, this return to the elementary which is one of the marks of a civilization in revolt against itself. It is no longer a question of recognizing appearances, by making a determined and conscious effort, but of no longer existing at all on the conscious level.

This remark applies its insight perfectly to Hawkes' fiction. One sees clearly his refusal to recognize, or abide, the rational consciousness in his fondness for withholding narrative information and in his habit of shuffling ordered events in time. He throws the map-hungry reader delicious bits of abusive, brilliant detail and will for pages toss out the false scents that send readers stumbling past his true authorial intentions like a shipwreck chasing his own footprints. His rigid consistency of tone and language leaves readers panting, breathless and dismayed.

He celebrates the game in which we are all imprisoned by our wishes to be free of rational consciousness. His comic treatment of violence, extreme detachment and crackling satire, thoughtful horrors driven through tangles of complex distortions—all combine to unsettle his reader, making him dependent on the author as a guide in this contrary and confusing landscape. Like Faulkner, Hawkes can gracefully subjugate his reader, and in this delightful violation of a reader's conventional trust is a measure of perverse satisfaction such as a Faulkner or a Flaubert must have enjoyed. How sad that many readers are unable to partake in the perverse pleasures which the novelist invites them to share.

But these considerations lead us away from the heart of the fiction, Hawkes' own heart of darkness. It seems wise to mention, however, that Hawkes' techniques and craftsmanship have earned him different tags and rubrics—"anti-novelist," "anti-realist," even, as one professor squeezed out, "a master of controlled incoherence." Like the effulgent "isms" of modern art, such labels take us only into the safety of speculation over literary schools.

Hawkes has, however, been lumped in with the French school of "anti-novelists," represented by Robbe-Grillet, Sarraute, Butor, Simon, Sapota, Duras, etc. Such references are spurious. The French authors, whose revolt is ostentatious and sentimental, are not anti-realists but intensified realists, minute regimentationists, pragmatic, seamless. Their revolt has roots in sociological, not literary, problems. They seem like children who reduce disobedience to the most superficial contrary acts of sulking behavior. Their distortions are so inconsistent, so haphazard, vibrant details and nuances of character rarely come across. And their revolt is doggedly stubborn and dull, all quite the opposite of Hawkes'.

His matchless disrespect for our habitual reading expectations has quite different an effect from that we experience by looking at a piece of bread from many angles for many pages. The difference is playfulness, humor, richness. The best method of expressing Hawkes' richness of language and conception would be to quote for pages. But anyone who has savored the indignant, haughty language of *The Owl* or *The Cannibal*, in which the author constantly undercuts Zizendorf's delightful pomposity, will understand Hawkes' ability to assume a voice and maintain it from cover to cover. The common rhythms of lower-class England are reproduced in *The Lime Twig* with a comic lilt that goes deeper than mere authenticity. The same is true of *The Beetle Leg*, with its dead twang of parody.

A similar depth and sensitivity breathes life into Hawkes' purely creative settings, landscapes with no real counterpart in the conscious world. They are so skillful a mixture of the real and the imagined that readers can barely notice any separations. In *The Cannibal*, the landscape was a suggestion of post-war Germany in ruins, a lifeless legacy of holocaust, decay, and dry copulation. It was a mythical, medieval kingdom cleft high in the Italian mountains in *The Owl*, a timeless landscape so barren that walls fell away from the proclamations pasted upon them. In *The Goose on the Grave*, Italy was again the setting, Italy stumbling through war, and in *The Beetle Leg*, vivid glimpses of the rutted American West with its corroded jail, roaming motorcyclists and suspicious ghosts of people moving over the useless dam in which a body is entombed.

The setting of *The Lime Twig* is also packed with significant detail, but the more easily followed narrative has been supported by a more realistic background—though the infernal steam bath, with its imps sloshing cold water from buckets, is a purely imaginative vision of Hell. In *Second Skin*, the modern setting shuttles between a curiously prehistoric Maine coast and the primitive, langorous pleasures of a tropical island that might be in the West Indies chain. Yet as various as these settings may appear, each possesses the particular kind of timeless violence that Hawkes injects into all his locations: "He brought back creation to the shores of the primeval seas where morality, as well as every other problem, loses all meaning," as Camus says of Lautréamont's Maldoror. The same is true of Hawkes, elemental and immoral.

The way in which readers experience a Hawkes narrative is equally elemental. Flannery O'Connor has said that one "suffers [*The Lime Twig*] like a dream." This is true of each of Hawkes' novels. His narratives move with the pace and color of a dream. Something in the dream reassures us; something either draws us on or repels us. Attraction or repulsion, these two violent reactions become suddenly mixed in the narrative as Hawkes writes it. A frustration, a tension, is created in which the reader finds it impossible to judge events and react as he would in consciousness. When Jacopo beats Edouard in the outdoor lavatory in *The Goose on the Grave,* the beating becomes a nightmarish dance, as if two figures were for a moment fatigued boxers, or marathon dancers, holding each other up in a dark, empty stadium.

Lucid colors of the dream are there: "It was true, his eyes did flash, and at one of the more painful blows—it grazed his eyelids—he took heart because he loved color." In this episode of pathetic comedy, the reader learns of Jacopo's presence in the lavatory just as Edouard does: a fragmentary shadow, glint of an ear-ring, odor of Jacopo's breath, a sinister figure heaving through the empty air that for a moment separates them. Silently, with agonizing slowness and deliberate hesitation, the narrative blossoms into a recognition of the fact that Jacopo is beating Edouard, for reasons unknown.

In each of Hawkes' "dreams" is this aspect of hallucination—a blank figure swimming into consciousness, still dream-like in its threat, materializing so indistinctly, we do not know whether to stand or bolt. The dream—what Hawkes calls "the mighty inner schism between the rational and the absurd"—carries in it our obsessions, what we hope and fear. Characters in *The Lime Twig* succumb to a mixture of what they hope for and fear, and readers who try to judge their deaths—Margaret mashed under Thick's rubber billy, Michael pulverized by the race horses, Hencher crushed by the ghostly, white stallion—are faced by the same frustration occasioned by the mixture of attraction and repulsion. Neither saved nor damned, Hawkes' characters are only human, figures to be given life by the author's malice or pity.

If we "suffer" the fiction as a dream, it can be argued, I think, that what we suffer most is the aftermath of the dream, the jarring recapitulation in consciousness, the cold creak of terror that does not disappear with opened eyes. For most of what we dream, we try to rationalize away. Hawkes does not. For him, the dream is the deeper reality; for the terror of experience, not ideas, is the only reality for the gothic writer. His aim is to make the dream a reality on paper without sacrificing its unconscious aspect of terror and indistinctness. What we feel moves us more than what we can prove.

The intense nightmare of *The Cannibal* or "Charivari" is steps away from the haunting narrative of *Second Skin* or *The Owl,* however. The insanity and corruption of characters in *The Beetle Leg,* though no less fierce, are less apparent than in *The Lime Twig,* in which the gangsters' calculated violence seems wittingly natural, easy, full of grace. Yet whatever the degree of terror, one can expect from Hawkes a fixed quantity, a spectrum across which the novelist slides his narrative like a scientist revving up the juice in electrodes in his patient's skull.

Obviously, the effect the aftermath of the dream has on a reader, depends on his personal insight and taste. Many readers absolutely wallow in the apparent grotesque of Hawkes' loving sacrifices—the chicken's head torn off, the female hostage slowly beaten to death, the dreamer trampled under flailing hooves, the child bitten by a rattlesnake and left virtually alone to die, the blind Pipistrello smashed and thrown from a cliff by a capricious boulder. The list could continue for pages. Projections of such naked horrors, made so palatable by the "demonic sympathy" and elegant detachment and diction, thrill readers abstractly, move them to admire Hawkes' subtle craftsmanship. But, says Hawkes, "mere malice is nothing in itself, of course, and the product of extreme fictive detachment is extreme fictive sympathy."

These same readers savored the coupling of a coward and an idiot in Faulkner's *The Hamlet,* or the dwarf taking into his mouth his injured fighting cock's head in *The Day of the Locust.* They cheered, perhaps, Maldoror's razor-slashed smile and the ingenious machine that serves up absurd retribution in "The Penal Colony." I suppose the unflinching gaze at purely creative horrors is what makes readers respond with admiration. Certainly, for pure, inventive evil and violence, one would search far to surpass Hawkes' slow description of the Duke cutting up his prey, a child, in *The Cannibal,* or his delicate narration of the brutal knifing of Fernando in *Second Skin.* But Hawkes' novels possess a deeper, less obvious violence, that which is undeclared and potential, like anxiety that hasn't yet the referent of a specific fear.

Extreme repugnance is the other extreme in reactions to Hawkes. A reader looks up from the episode in *The Beetle Leg* in which Luke hooks a bloated foetus—"God's naked child"—floating in the river, a flaccid bag of unformed guts, and threatens to be sick on the floor: A common reaction to the less palatable horrors of Mr. Hawkes. And surely, both the delight and the revulsion, macabre enjoyment or frank disgust, are entirely compatible with the author's intentions. In each sacrifice is a challenge to the reader to enter into the spirit of the saved and the damned alike. The banality of revulsion, in such a case, is a saving grace.

Sacrifices abound in *The Cannibal,* for example, where readers find their sympathies challenged in astonishing ways. First of all, Germany itself has been sacrificed in a cannibal feast of pride and violence. The "institution" has no function; for the living inhabitants, less lively than the ghosts of this landscape, simply prey on each other in a larger, undeclared institution. Freedom is a worthless caprice. Morality has been bombed out and one man devours his fellow without a hint of rational remorse or disgust.

In this atmosphere, murder and suicide, love and violence lose the distinction of differences. Only primeval urges reign and every question of morality is a dead issue. None of this is explained by the wars, which occur vaguely, a plane which happens to drop into the street killing Stella's mother, the American agent, Leevey, on his motorcycle. It is not history that concerns Hawkes but only its effects that fill the skull of a single character. He shrinks the world, as Guerard suggested, into the skull of one man or woman; the "mass plague" becomes the single experience. The same compression is evident in *The Owl,* in which the fascism of tyrants from antiquity to the present is reflected in the hangman's control over his ironclad monarchy, Sasso Fetore. He controls marriage, death–life.

And in these "worlds" where everything is subject to control and sacrifice, everything is subject to terror. In such a condition, anxiety balloons, and the distinction between what one hopes for and fears, once more, becomes almost pathologically similar. The distorted merging of past and present in *The Cannibal* helps produce this disturbance. Finally a reader must accept it and allow himself to be increasingly led by the hand through these curious landscapes that grow less absurd the longer he inhabits them. By mixing time and conceiving from a viewpoint of extreme distortion, Hawkes forces upon us a fiction to be felt rather than talked about intellectually. He gives power to his voice and surely shares in the might enjoyed by characters such as the hangman, Cap Leech, Zizendorf, Larry.

In *Second Skin,* the roving, amorphous band of wicked potential that were dogs in *The Cannibal* has become a trio of hard-nosed Maine fishermen. The inhuman motorcycles of *The Beetle Leg* Red Devils become hot-rod automobiles. Undeclared evil, potential violence–these are Hawkes' concerns as he describes the masterful Kissin' Bandits of Company C, AWOL soldiers who descend on the narrator, Skipper, and his daughter after their bus is wrecked in the desert. They hold the father and daughter at gun-point, strip off their uniforms–but leave on helmets–and steal kisses from Cassandra. One expects them to rape her on the spot, and it is a delightful irony that moved Hawkes to create such a humorous violation of Skipper's affection for his daughter.

His humor is similar in the scene during which Skipper, in Maine, is lured from a dance out into the snow and pelted by the fishermen and the sadistic Miranda with snowballs. Fat, a wheezing kind of Walter Mitty, Skipper is blessed with a preciosity and sentimentality. Sexless, withdrawn, neither father nor lover, he guards his daughter with a pathetic kind of loyalty and passion. The fishermen, Bub, Jomo and Red take turns at Cassandra, while the candor of their evil fills Skipper with a paralyzing horror.

They threaten him with a conscienceless wit and singleness of purpose he cannot possess. In Skipper, Hawkes has articulated much of the indistinct estrangement that kept his readers so distant from Il Gufo. Skipper seems to be Hencher in a naval uniform. Of course, as Larry and his mob went scot free in *The Lime Twig,* the fishermen go scot free in *Second Skin.* Those who come by evil naturally go unpunished in Hawkes' world, where society's "disruptive needs" cannot be reconciled with society's morality. The disruptive needs create their own morality–or the lack of it–and this is the nightmare to be faced which looms constantly in Hawkes' novels. The dogs, the Red Devils, the fishermen in their infernal hot-rod, the rolling boulder that crushes Pipistrello, the phallus-God of Larry and his mob—these are the obsessions, bestial puzzles, portents of malice and indifference, that haunt the fiction of John Hawkes. They are brilliant fictional images of our unmanageable existence, the events and personalities we can never tame to our wishes. They roam in these ruined landscapes and lives with a particular abandon, untamable and enviable, as well as frightful and pitiable.

The mixture of pity and exhilaration in the human condition is recreated with chilling authenticity by Hawkes, who, speaking about the writing of Djuna Barnes, neatly described his own: "Surely there is unpardonable distinction in this kind of writing, a certain incorrigible assumption of a prophetic role in reverse, when the most baffling of unsympathetic attitudes is turned upon the grudges, guilts and renunciations harbored in the tangled seepage of our earliest recollections and originations."

Certainly, Hawkes' laughter is Maldoror's laughter of a mouth slashed by a razor. His is a search into the pit that stops at no amount of terrifying discovery. He is into everything and if there is confusion and blackness in his truth, then it is up to us to find out why, to discover with him both the wit and the blackness in which we all unconsciously partake. His disturbances are those that start cracks creeping out in every human spirit, and perhaps the acceptance of such disturbances will save the spirit from crumbling completely. Admitting everything, rejecting nothing, Hawkes writes from a viewpoint held by few American authors.

In *The Beetle Leg,* the Red Devils, black centaurs in the night, career through the dead town and streak off into the darkness on their motorcycles. In wonderment a young boy exclaims, "They had jewels all over them!"

"We don't want to hear about it," replies Luke Lampson.

I believe that states the purpose for which John Hawkes writes.

Lucy Frost

Awakening Paradise

"Queequeg was a native of Kokovoko, an island far away to the West and South. It is not down in any map; true places never are."

—"Biographical," *Moby Dick,* Ch. 12

Little about the novels of John Hawkes, including their subject matter, is immediately clear when one begins reading them. The reader of *Second Skin*

Lucy Frost teaches at La Trobe University in Melbourne.

faces a narrative shifting chapter by chapter from readily recognizable locations in California and the eastern seaboard to an island which, the narrator repeatedly insists, "*is* a wandering island, of course, unlocated in space and quite out of time"(46).[1] Understandably, readers feel baffled. If the wandering island is imaginary, are the other sections of the book which seem realistic also imaginary, or at least hallucinatory? Or, if their reality is granted, what is one to make of the narrator? Is he insane? If so, how is his narrative to be read? Without some answer to such questions, the reader of *Second Skin* is stranded in confusion.

The novel's techniques alienate some readers. Plot, character, setting, and theme may be aspects of most novels, but Hawkes has said that he began writing fiction in conscious rebellion against them, believing them "the true enemies of the novel." He sees his novels as carefully wrought works with structures of "verbal and psychological coherence." This coherence is attained by means of "related or corresponding event, recurring image and recurring action."[2] Using these techniques based on juxtaposition and recurrence, Hawkes conveys a sense of violent discordance in life without denying unity to his art. This is of utmost importance, for violent discordance is at the heart of the subject matter throughout his fiction. A reader who is willing to accept Hawkes' techniques while reading *Second Skin* will be able to discover what is going on in the novel, to perceive a unity from which meaning and significance emerge. He will also notice that *Second Skin* does have a public level of experience which the reader can share with the novelist. The reader may not like what he finds on this level, but he will certainly see that *Second Skin* can be read as a vision of the life he is living.

One recurring action which provides structural unity for the entire novel is the voyage. Some of the novel's voyages are literal journeys over the ocean. More are metaphoric, events made voyages by images, context, and pattern. When the narrative is seen as interlocking voyages, the existence of the "imaginary island" may cause the reader less difficulty. That island can be approached as the narrator approaches it, in the context established by the voyages preceding his arrival on its shores. Although the name of the narrator is "Edward," he is usually referred to as "Skipper," and the voyage during which he is literally a "Skipper" provides a prototype by which episodes preceding Cassandra's death can be shaped into the pattern of a voyage.

During this literal voyage, as Skipper later remembers, "I suffered each separate moment of my personal contribution to the obscene annals of naval history"(52). The particular annals are those of World War II, a period in recent American history when forces later concealed or obscured were clearly

---

[1]Each page reference to *Second Skin* (New York, 1963) is given in parentheses after the quotation.

[2]"John Hawkes: an Interview," *Wisconsin Studies in Contemporary Literature,* VI (1965), 149.

visible. The war can function as a metaphor for an entire society, as an accusation against that society; the goals of a nation mobilized for war are destruction and death. These goals are Skipper's personal antagonists, and without the wartime setting, Skipper's personal struggle would be private. In Hawkes' treatment, Skipper becomes a representative man, his struggle emblematic.

The terms of Skipper's struggle are defined during a mutiny aboard his ship. As naval captain, Skipper performs disastrously because he does not keep his mind on his work. He becomes so involved with spiritual matters that his days are absorbed by reading the Bible and assisting the Chaplain in "giving to each man his short ration of mysterious life"(139). Because Skipper never again seems in the least interested in religion, his preoccupation at this point may appear odd. But it is consistent with the identity he claims for himself in the novel's opening chapter. Although the chapter is entitled "Naming Names," Skipper names other characters in his narrative but not himself. Instead of naming his own name, he begins in the novel's first sentences by introducing himself as a lover:

> I will tell you in a few words who I am: lover of the hummingbird that darts to the flower beyond the rotted sill where my feet are propped; lover of bright needlepoint and the bright stitching fingers of humorless old ladies bent to their sweet and infamous designs; lover of parasols made from the same puffy stuff as a young girl's underdrawers; still lover of that small naval boat which somehow survived the distressing years of my life between her decks or in her pilothouse; and also lover of poor dear black Sonny, my mess boy, fellow victim and confidant, and of my wife and child. But, most of all, lover of my harmless and sanguine self.(1)

As a self-professed, all-embracing lover, Skipper is committed to preserving the object of his love: life. He is a servant of what Freud called Eros, and as such he does battle with the antagonist of Eros, Thanatos. It is this battle that he is fighting aboard his ship, and this battle is not consonant with his public, social role. To be a naval captain participating in his nation's organized pursuit of death through acts of war is inappropriate for a man serving Eros, so Skipper happily ministers to the wounded but does not himself wound. The actual chores of captaincy he relinquishes to his first mate, "my devil, Tremlow"(5), who in turn fulfills his duties by leading a mutiny against a captain lost in spiritual meditation. Even as the victim of murderous, sexually perverted Tremlow, Skipper does not retaliate, does not strike back in the dialectic with Thanatos. As constantly happens in the incidents leading up to Cassandra's death, Skipper will struggle on in the daily battle against his foes, but in a crisis he is impotent, a grotesque and comic failure. After he is saved by the terrified Chaplain who foils the mutineers' design, Skipper watches Tremlow escape with his cohorts in three life boats:

And perhaps I should have unlimbered one of the three-inch guns and ordered them picked off. It would have been easy. And they deserved it. But I lay on the deck . . . I let them go. Merely watched and wondered what the sun would do to Tremlow in that grass skirt, wondered what he would say when he was picked up. . . . And later, much later, I reported the group of them to be missing in action and told the old man we lost the boats in a storm.(148)

Skipper's experience as a literal captain forms a pattern repeated in other experiences he undergoes before he arrives at the wandering island. Always he undertakes the service of Eros; in that service he is buffeted about by the forces of death, and in whatever he seeks to do, he fails. But whereas Tremlow's mutiny simply humiliates him, Cassandra's death defeats him utterly. The chronicle Skipper writes on the sunny island is the history of his defeat.

The chronicle begins with a land journey across the American continent— "our ill-fated trip across the southwestern wartime desert of the United States"(46)—in a bus which Skipper describes as having a "long steel body like a submarine"(26), a bus filled with sailors, Skipper, his daughter, and granddaughter. For Skipper the bus trip is the first part of a journey of "ten months during which I attempted to prolong Cassandra's life, ten subtle months of my final awakening"(5). The destination of the voyage through space, and the beginning of the voyage through time is what Skipper hopes will be a "gentle Island" in the Atlantic. The move to the Atlantic island represents in geographical terms Skipper's attempt to preserve Cassandra's life by removing her from an environment permeated by death, where on his last shore patrol in New York City, "this wartime capital of the world"(44), he had found his daughter's homosexual husband strangled with the strings of his guitar. As one might predict from these gruesome preparatory incidents, the island turns out to be a severe disappointment. Nothing gentle has much chance to survive unscathed on this island in the black Atlantic. The essence of the island is crystallized in the character of Miranda, the treacherous widow who persuades Skipper to ignore "my mistrust of the nautical life, the suspicion of my tendency toward seasickness, the uneasiness I had come to feel in the presence of small boats whether in or out of the water" (174), and to go for an excursion on the *Peter Poor*. By doing so, he gives over control of his voyage to Captain Red and sails with Cassandra on a final voyage into the seas of death, for—as he realizes later—that boat trip initiated a chain of events culminating inevitably in Cassandra's death and, with it, his own defeat: ". . . I know now that there was a chance for Cassandra up to the very

moment she swung her foot gaily over the rail of the *Peter Poor* and stood
with her hair blowing and her skirt blowing on the cluttered deck of that
water-logged tub of Red's. But there was no chance really for Cassandra after
that. No chance at all. The second of the four seasons sucked her under, the
sea was cruel"(175).

Skipper fails precisely because the cruelty is in the sea and what man can
battle such a foe? A man can gain some protection from the water when it is
only rain or spray, because then an oil skin coat, the "second skin" of the
title, is adequate. But when the menacing wind unleashes the sea's cruelty,
those second skins are worthless. By depending heavily on the sea and the
wind as explanations for Cassandra's death, by implicating Miranda, Captain
Red, Jomo, and Bub, and then by having Cassandra kill herself, Hawkes
insists to the reader that no lucid analysis of the relationship between victim
and assailant is possible here. With the assailant so elusive, the victim will
perish in spite of all the protective measures another may make in his behalf.
In such a world, Skipper can never be a successful lover. All round him people
are dying in spite of his passionate attempts to keep them on the ship, to
keep them protected by oil skins from the menacing wind, to retain control
over life, over the ship. Contrary to the ideas he has inherited through the
secular channels of Western humanism, Skipper discovers in heartbreaking
experiences that love will not save the world when love entails perpetual
suffering—and nothing but suffering.

The episode culminating in Cassandra's death in turn creates the pattern
unifying the scattered but pervasive references to Skipper's earlier life. These
patterns are not apparent when one is reading the novel straight through.
Episodes are abruptly cut, to be picked up chapters later. References are
made to people and events not explained at all until, by bits and pieces, the
reader gathers enough information to put them together. Various techniques
keep the reader bewildered, pressing upon him a feeling that the fictional
world being created as he reads apparently does not make sense. Given the
novel's subject matter, these novelistic devices have philosophical implications: they suggest that human life, caught in a dialectical tension between
the forces of Eros and Thanatos, has no underlying order in itself. Men give it
an order through the forms of their culture, but only if the forms are
celebrations of Eros. If they serve Thanatos, the forms serve those demonic
forces characterized by their movement toward disintegration.

When Skipper escapes the culture oriented toward the demonic, Hawkes
alters the pattern of his voyage. The new pattern is created by means of
allusions to *The Tempest,* providing Hawkes with the conventions of the
pastoral romance in which two ordinarily distinct worlds can be bridged. A
reader who has accepted the boat trip from Milan to Prospero's island has an
imaginative context in which to understand Skipper's leap from New Jersey
to the wandering island out of space and time. Both voyages are undertaken

by betrayed men who have fallen victim to societies that cast them out; both voyages lead to Edenic islands where the victims recover control over life around them, where they recover their own sense of dignity, where life is serene and nature beneficent. Skipper, however, is not Prospero: "I was tossed up spent and half-naked on the invisible shore of our wandering island—old Ariel in sneakers, sprite surviving in bald-headed man of fair complexion . . ."(162). The association with Ariel certainly reinforces some of Skipper's aspirations, even though at the same time comically undercutting this earthbound sprite. In terms of the narrative, the association suggests the release of this sprite from his torment by "the foul witch Sycorax." That witch is never named in *Second Skin*, but just as she enslaved Shakespeare's Ariel on the island before Prospero arrived, so she has enslaved Skipper on "the gentle island." In keeping with his pervasive techniques of irony, Hawkes names Skipper's witch "Miranda." As Skipper writes later, the name "Miranda" embodied "the very music of charity, innocence, obedience, love"(5). But the Miranda he met was.his antagonist, not his salvation: "No one could have given a more ugly denial to that heartbreaking and softly fluted name than the tall and treacherous woman"(5). Seeking a fairy godmother to preserve his princess, he has found instead the wicked witch who guzzles whiskey at six in the morning while listening to the *Horst Wessel* song on a phonograph in an enchanted room complete with spinning wheel; who wards off asthmatic attacks by breathing in "the fumes of the witches' pot"(67); who cuts the top off the nipples for Pixie's bottles and pours the milk down the sink; and who at last—after a series of preparatory episodes, all designed to destroy Skipper's command—helps distract the frantic father while his daughter is held captive in the lighthouse—"princess, poor princess and her tower"(58)—and jumps to her death. As a present to the grieving father, Miranda then presents Skipper with a gaily wrapped package which she assures him contains the foetus explaining Cassandra's death. Without opening the package to see, Skipper takes it and Pixie out to the cemetery where he buries it on the top of Cassandra's grave. After this, he leaves the island of death and like Ariel is released from the witch. Another pilgrimage to a cemetery occurs at the conclusion of the novel. The contrast between the two pilgrimages repeats the contrast between the two voyages.

While the allusions to *The Tempest* establish the pattern for a new voyage ending in triumph rather than defeat, the effects of the previous voyages are kept before the reader's eyes by means of the details describing Skipper's condition when he arrives at the island. The picture of Skipper washed onto the shore translates into visual, physical terms his invisible state at the end of the ten months' effort to save Cassandra's life and at the end of the fifty years' effort to save lives all around him. Skipper is "tossed" up. No longer even attempting to command, he is without any ship and is at the mercy of powers beyond him, as he has always been but had never recognized until "his final awakening" at the time of Cassandra's death. He is "spent and half-naked." These adjectives remind the reader that before Skipper was Ariel, he was a man clothed in a "second skin."[3] The "second skin" of the title is mentioned only once in the novel, in a remark made by Skipper when he sets off on that fatal voyage of the *Peter Poor.* "Second skin" refers to the oil skin coat given Skipper as protection against the wind, rain, and rough seas. The protection is inadequate, for Skipper gets sick, vomits, then passes out for most of the trip. Vomiting becomes a powerful, if odd, image for the progress this pilgrim makes to the end of nihilism: "Anyone who has gotten down on his knees to vomit has discovered, if only by accident, the position of prayer"(127). At the limit of what is physically bearable, the body rebels, and Skipper's entire life has led him to the emotional and psychological limits of what a human can bear before rebellion. He is the son of an undertaker; a member of a family of suicides within a nation at war; an inheritor of a civilization which gives him no forms for preserving life—his playing Brahms on his cello in a vain attempt to save his father from shooting himself is perhaps the clearest image of what happens over and over. At last Skipper is beaten helpless into a corner where other members of his family had been, too. They killed themselves; he vomits. Within this context of suicides, Skipper's vomiting becomes ironically a source of hope. Suicide is an act of physical violence that achieves its end when man is reduced to matter. Vomiting is an act of physical violence which leads beyond the violence itself to the position of prayer and ultimately to the man washed ashore without his oil skin coat, spent but not drowned.

The novel as a whole also prepares a public dimension for this image of Skipper as Ariel. Second skins are those protective devices prepared by men who attempt to ward off the assailing forces of Thanatos. Skipper has prepared many from the time he played Brahms to his father, to the time he takes Cassandra to the "gentle island" in the Atlantic. But the assailing forces are beyond any single man's control, as the wind imagery makes clear throughout the novel. When explaining his "true subject"(3) for his "naked history"(9) in the opening chapter, Skipper the chronicler suggests first that the subject may be the wind, and in one sense it surely is. Wind becomes a metaphor for powers controlling the external world in which any self must exist. Since it cannot be seen, held, or controlled, wind is an impersonal assailant of the victim, man. Wearing an oil skin coat to ward off the effects

---

[3]*Moby-Dick* seems to have provided a source for Hawkes' use of this image: "To be sure, in coolish weather you may carry your house aloft with you, in the shape of a watch-coat; but properly speaking the thickest watch-coat is no more of a house than the unclad body; for as the soul is glued inside of its fleshly tabernacle, and cannot freely move about in it, nor even more out of it, without running great risk of perishing (like an ignorant pilgram crossing the snowy Alps in winter); so a watch-coat is not so much of a house as it is a mere envelope, or additional skin encasing you."—"The Mast-head," *Moby-Dick.*

of the wind is only surface protection, inadequate against an assailant able to destroy the foundations of stability in one's environment by tossing the boat itself. The wind, blowing both breezes and gales, can "alter the flavor of our inmost recollections of pleasure or pain . . ."(3). So long as man lives in an environment of extremes, he will be victim to pain. So long as Skipper is on the Atlantic island he will be victimized by the painful gales. But when he gets to his wandering island, he can walk enveloped in the wind. So moderate is the climate that he need wear no clothes. Returning to the simplicity of the body on this sunny island requires an abstraction from the human extremes which characterize not just twentieth-century civilization, but all civilization. Skipper, the only white man in his black paradise, is completely isolated from his own, white civilization, past and present nor is a highly sophisticated civilization ever likely to exist here. Days are too warm, life too lazy, the wind too consistently gentle. The image of Skipper as Ariel tossed on the shore "spent and half-naked" is an image of the moment of metamorphosis when death becomes rebirth, but only in a post-cultural environment where the cultural forms inherited from Europe and existing there and in the United States have ceased operating altogether.

A constant source of violence and death in John Hawkes' earlier novels is the continued use of the cultural forms that simply do not fulfill the desires of men and as a result arouse hatred where there might have been love. In other words, the forms make room only for an expression of man's death instinct, for Thanatos. This is also the situation in the sections of *Second Skin* which Skipper writes as his chronicle. But in the sections comprising time present, the sections dealing with the wandering island, the situation is different *because* the forms traditional to Western culture exert no power over the lives of the characters. Secular culture of the past is represented by buildings. At the decaying plantation house Skipper writes with his feet propped on the "rotted sill." The mill is now a scene of rendezvous for lovers and not of work in this un-American paradise with no vestiges of island industry such as Skipper noticed on Miranda's island. Sacred culture is represented by "little Sister Josie"(49), who continues only the Christian traditions glorifying life, unlike Dolce—in Hawkes' earlier novel *The Goose on the Grave*—with his penchant for the suffering Christ and for creating martyrs himself. Sister Josie "attends all our births" and "vicariously shares the joys of pregnancy"(49) with Catalina Kate. References to the civilization which Skipper has left are invariably comic. Kate's announcement of her pregnancy, for example, is accompanied by a gift to Skipper and Sonny, "a present with which to celebrate the happy news, a pound of American hot dogs wrapped up in a moldy and dog-eared sheet of soggy newspaper"(49). Rendering Skipper's original world comic, Hawkes renders it non-violent and reduces it to harmlessness—but only because Skipper's voyage has removed him from it. The perspective, not the world, has changed.

Western culture, as Hawkes treats it throughout his fiction, is making a concerted drive toward violent destruction and death. The hope expressed in *Second Skin* is for a life in which cultural forms perpetuate the values of Eros. Analysis in these terms suggests that Hawkes is molding his fictional worlds into much the same shape as that created by Norman O. Brown in *Life Against Death* and *Love's Body*. The two writers, probably unknown to each other, analyze our world in strikingly similar terms: Life (Eros) is locked in a struggle with death (Thanatos) and is losing in today's Western culture. Both writers envisage the same way out: there must be a resurrection of love's body, for only then—as Christian theology once recognized—can life be reconciled with death. This resurrection is the organizing principle for the portrayal of Skipper's paradise. At the heart of the paradise is sex, which Brown calls "the prototype of all opposition or contrariety." The prototype of the resolution uniting the opposing principles is coitus. Coitus unhampered by repressive moral and social forms has been associated in the Western mind with island paradises ever since the sailors of Wallis, Bougainville, and Cook delighted in the gifts of Tahiti late in the eighteenth century. In Skipper's mind the association of coitus and paradise is made specifically a resolution of the irreconcilable animosity between the lover and Miranda, the dominant female on the first island. Skipper associates Miranda with that part of his life set in the context of death, and Kate with that part in the context of life through love's body:

> Now I have Catalina Kate instead. And this—Sonny and I both agree—this is love. Here I have only to drop my trousers—no shirt, no undershirt, no shorts—to awaken paradise itself, awaken it with the sympathetic sound of Catalina Kate's soft laughter. And it makes no difference at all. Because I am seven years away from Miranda, seven years from that first island—black, wet, snow-swept in a deep relentless sea—and seven years from Cassandra's death and, thanks to the wind, the gold, the women and Sonny and my new profession, am more in love than ever. Until now the cemetery has been my battleground. But no more. Perhaps even my father, the dead mortician, would be proud of me.(46-47)

Clearly on this island where "I have only to drop my trousers . . . to awaken paradise itself" Skipper can put an end to his previous strife with the external world and can enjoy his identity as lover.

But just as Hawkes traps his characters in public hells, so he places Skipper in a public paradise. Granted, the public is small—Sonny, Kate, Sister Josie and Big Bertha. Its number will increase. Indeed, they do so with the birth of the baby. To extend to those people the values of his paradise, Skipper consciously transforms the events of life into the rituals marking the forms that constitute a culture. Hawkes makes the act of transformation explicit when he has Skipper design new forms to cultivate those values emanating from Eros. The private act of coitus becomes the center of a religious celebration that takes the form of a fertility cult. In addition to celebrating present life, the rites assure the future. This is important to Skipper, for whom coitus alone is inadequate. Love must bring life; coitus, pregnancy. This explains why Skipper is the center of the fertility rites instead of Kate, the potential great earth mother. Kate can only produce one child at a time, whereas Skipper can engender life on a much larger scale. And he is not confined to human life: "...I am much esteemed as the man who inseminates the cows and causes these enormous soft animals to bring forth calves"(47). It is this new giver of life that Sister Josie, the little black nun remaining from the old order, now follows. At Skipper's command, Josie, Sonny, and Catalina Kate follow their new leader, descendent of "those little black seeds of death"(161), as he goes to implant "the seeds of life" in a desiring cow: "... I, Skipper, led the way. I knew the way, was the man in charge—the A1—and there was no mistaking me for anything but the leader now, and they were faithful followers, my entourage"(166).

But this paradise is public only *inside* the novel. It is not likely to bear any resemblance to the world as the reader knows it. Only as art does the imaginary island out of space and time join the world of space and time and become "true," in Melville's sense. Hawkes establishes a comic association between the A1 and a novelist by having Skipper write a book when not busy impregnating Kate or cows, and when not constructing rituals. By means of the novelist's wonderfully inventive—his fertile—imagination, the reader receives the seeds of life through the artificial method that is art. If the A1 is successful, the reader will become the impregnated cow.

Because the synthesis between Skipper's desires and his external world has taken place on an imaginary island, the form of the novel raises those questions that I asked at the outset about reality in the world of *Second Skin,* and about the reader's response to Skipper's narrative. In the first question, the central issue is that of locating reality. How can both the sections on and off the wandering island be considered real? How can the reader move from what seems to be one type of reality to another within the novel, when he certainly cannot in life? In my reading of the novel, I have accepted Skipper's implied perception of both environments as real, as physical places where he lives. To him the environments are distinct in the quality of life available but not in their degree of reality. This is not true for the reader, of course, and that leads to the second question about the reader's response to Skipper's narrative. The reader cannot get onto that wandering island physically, as Skipper did. But he can get onto it imaginatively if he will accept the kind of reality available in art which does not aim at realism in the narrow sense. It might be possible to remove the problems by calling *Second Skin* a "fantasy" or a "fable," but I prefer to avoid the problem of defining such terms and to suggest instead that the form of *Second Skin* has much in common with the form of *The Tempest* and *Gulliver's Travels*. In all three works voyages are made from places listed in geography books to places existing only within the works of art themselves. This kind of movement, then, is a traditional literary convention and need not baffle the reader unduly. Hawkes himself, as I have suggested, establishes his links to this convention by means of the direct allusions to *The Tempest*.

The association with *Gulliver's Travels* exists not within the novel, but as a critical perspective. From this perspective the reader can see the relationship of the wandering island to his own anchored continent. Both Book IV of *Gulliver's Travels* and *Second Skin* are finally ironic. Gulliver certainly wanted to stay in that land of the Houyhnhnms where he found his utopia, just as Skipper is content to remain on his sunny isle, basking in his utopia. And the land of the Houyhnhnms, no matter how ironically treated by Swift, is undoubtedly the imaginary land in which Swift, too, thought that he would enjoy spending his days conversing intelligently with rational beings far away from Ireland. Swift, mocking Gulliver, mocks himself, but not his desires. Like Gulliver, he is a man, and so must be forced back into his native land where the stench of the yahoos is almost more than he can bear. Hawkes, too, treats his utopian island ironically. In contrast, however, to the grim and bitter irony pervading the bleak "lunar landscapes" of his earlier novels and also pervading those sections of *Second Skin* set in time and space, the irony with which Skipper's sunny isle is treated is decidedly comic and sympathetic. On a grant from the Guggenheim Foundation, Hawkes escaped from the eastern United States to spend a year on a Carribean island writing a novel about a bumbling, loving man on a similar island who is writing a record of life which reads much like those earlier records in Hawkes' fiction from *Charivari* through *The Lime Twig*. In so far as Skipper's battle against the forces of death is the central battle throughout Hawkes' fiction, the release from the burdens of this battle can, I think, be read as a utopian state and its terms be taken seriously on a thematic level.

This battle against the forces of death is Hawkes' form of the motif running through all literature that chronicles man's recognition of evil and his attempts to move beyond this recognition. The movement beyond is necessary if evil is not to be final in an author's vision, if Zizendorf (*The Cannibal*), and the Sheriff (*The Beetle Leg*), and Dolce (*The Goose on the Grave*), and Miranda, are not to have final say. For the battle to end in victory it is necessary to get away from a landscape in which Thanatos is stronger than Eros, evil than good. Skipper has made this escape. As Hawkes said, speaking of the novel in an interview, Skipper "comes out of a world of suicide." At first he is submerged in that world and indeed "the drama in the novel, the conflict in the novel, is the narrator's effort to prevent his daughter's suicide . . . ." Although he fails in this effort, and although "he himself undergoes all kinds of tribulations and violations . . . by the end of the novel, I think we do have, in effect, a survivor. This is the first time, I think, in my fiction that there is something affirmative." Hawkes' comments on the terms of the survival are particularly interesting in light of the reading I have been proposing: ". . . even I got very much involved in the life-force versus death. The life and death in the novel go on as a kind of equal contest, until the very end, when a new-born baby, perhaps the narrator's, is taken to a cemetery on a tropical island, on an imaginary island, really, taken to a cemetery on All Saints' Eve with the candles lighted on the graves . . . ."[4] At the end of a voyage, the voyager has awakened paradise within himself and his world. Skipper's movement through the episodes of the voyage to the awakening at the end has provided a narrative unity for the novel. The voyage has been made in public terms so that the predicament of Skipper has become Hawkes' vision of the predicament of any American today. Only the awakening is private, belonging to Skipper alone; and yet even here it is public on an abstract level since the desires of Skipper and the vision of a world governed by Eros evoke a response in so many various people now trapped in a violent, destructive civilization.

William R. Robinson

John Hawkes' Artificial Inseminator

The most readily apparent quality of John Hawkes' *Second Skin* is its tropical luxuriance—the lush, ebullient, resplendent energy that bountifully gushes out through its style. In this way, above all, Hawkes fulfills the promise of his narrator's claim to being a lover and to triumphing courageously over death. But a truer appreciation of the narrator's gift—in both senses of the word: as his given vitality and as the testament of his life offered to the world in the form of a book—as Hawkes' accomplishment—can be gained through the numerous literary correlates that immediately spring to mind in even a casual reading of the book.

The first in order of appearance, figuratively alluded to in the title, is with the metamorphical tradition. Hawkes explicitly connects his narrative with

---

[4] John Graham, "John Hawkes on his Novels," *The Massachusetts Review,* VII (Summer 1966), 459.
William R. Robinson is associate professor of English at the University of Florida, Gainesville.

the current of "pastoral"(166)[1] that flows through Ovid and Shakespeare and
the Romantics and bears nature's miraculous, phoenix-like capacity to renew
itself perpetually from its self-inflicted death. *Second Skin,* drawing its
exuberant existence from this tradition, reenacts this tradition's creation
myth. With this difference: its narrator-protagonist, Skipper, undergoes an
ironic metamorphosis. He can watch "the sensual brown metamorphosis in
my thin cup"(201) of coffee, a pseudo-metamorphosis since no substantial
change occurs, only an illusory one, but he himself eludes what he regards as
his father's intention, in committing suicide, that he "undergo some sort of
transformation"(2). He never radically alters his direction or aspiration; he
remains from first to last a constant, indestructable human identity. His
overtly acknowledged second skin is not the serpent's iridescent new one that
cracks and sloughs off the dead old one in the expansive growth of its life. It
is, rather, a too small "oilskin"(180)—that is, materials of nature shaped by
man as an outer covering to protect his life against the rough sea when he is
vulnerable to the inhuman element. His second skin protects his "especially
sensitive" skin from the wind, in other words, from metamorphosis, from a
radical change whereby he would become something less or more or other
than what he is as a man—a pure soul, a transcendent spirit, a crude physical
creature such as Red, Miranda, or Jomo, or simply dead. Under its protection
he clarifies himself; he liberates and becomes what he inherently is.

After this initial correlate—now selecting at random—*Second Skin* shares
the literary bed of such modern works as *Zorba the Greek, The Horse's
Mouth* (whose protagonist is Gulley Jimson), and *Henderson the Rain King.*
The fifty-nine year old Skipper, perennially youthful while maturely wise in
the way of life, isn't exactly "a dirty old man." But his indefatigable will to
live and his abundant sensuality qualify him to rank among these modern
Falstaffian heroes. Maybe with his island for his dominion there is a touch
more in him of Prospero, the ruling spirit (though for a while encumbered by
an ironic Miranda), than the others, yet his six feet and 200 pounds of flesh
make him, like them, a solid creature of this world and his powers no more
than the powers of life. So in addition to being an ironic version of
metamorphosis story, Hawkes' novel—besides being an ironic version of *The
Tempest*—belongs to a distinctly modern prose narrative genre that cultivates
the complex interrelation of the spiritual and the physical or, in short, the
created and creative condition. And its hero characteristically combines
youth's zest with experience's energy and practicality.

This genre, however, historically connects with and continues a long
tradition of comedy in English literature dating back to Chaucer. In that
tradition, as probably in all comedy, a good genie saves the world from
catastrophe, comedy being miracle, the inexplicable redemption of life that

---

[1] All references are to *Second Skin* (New York: New Directions, 1964).

frees it from the clutches of death; tragedy, on the other hand, has as its domain the necessity existence suffers from, as exemplified by growth and aging, to grind out mercilessly its inevitable, "programmed" course in time to doom. That genie in Chaucer is a built-in self-corrective rational principle that keeps discordant passions from knocking life off balance. In Shakespeare, the genie enters the staggering world, like Christian grace, from outside it—as when the stranger Viola saves Illyria from its love sickness unto death in *Twelfth Night.* For Fielding the genie of reason, an *a priori* law of spirit, presides benignly in *Tom Jones* over the rambunctious passions, seeing to it that they play within the rules, which are rather relaxed but never enough to let the passions get out of bounds. Realism and naturalism—the nineteenth century after Dickens—clanked along mechanically toward its exhaustion. But the resurrected genie of the twentieth century's extravagant comedy emerges from Hawkes' magic lamp in its characteristic form of rampant life, once again, as in Chaucer, inherent but not so cautiously reined in by reason.

Reason, in fact, assumes a role decidedly subordinate to life. Its reduced position is perhaps most overtly signaled by the romance correlate. *Second Skin,* by self-admission(162, 173) traces its lineage from that ancestry perhaps more insistently than any other kinship. Among its inheritances from this source can be counted the liberties of dealing in "the truths of the human heart" (Hawthorne's definition of its province, of course, in distinguishing the romance from the novel), its subject of love, and its venturing upon the high seas—the favorite locale of the nineteenth-century romance. Hawkes works many twists upon his Romantic heritage but none more significant than his repudiation of the sea as that great mystic solvent in which Whitman, for example, bathed his cosmic imagination. As with the metamorphic tradition, he turns the Romantic ironically against itself and disciplines fantasy into vitalistic and humanistic art.

Other correlates, though less explicitly evident in the narrative, come readily to mind—such as the one connecting *Second Skin* with Ibsen's joy of life and Neitzsche's and Shaw's life force or narratives of post-war resurgence such as Albert Camus' *The Plague.* But those mentioned testify sufficiently to Hawkes' self-consciousness literariness. What is most important about them is that with their deliberate display he focuses attention upon the artifice of his art. As he also does with his artificially designed plot structure. Skipper, who can and does skip, along the surface and from one plane to another, insists that he, as "the man in charge"(166), maintains mastery of his craft, whether it be his boat, island, or narrative. Similarly, Hawkes makes his light fantastic dance to his imagination's time by managing chronology to suit his "analytical" purpose, which is to center toward the crucial turning point in Skipper's career and the matrix of his art. As master of time and change, he weaves together a counterpoint of "dead time"(89)—"the time that swept us all away"(19), the time of "dead reckoning"(162)—and "the time of no time"(e.g., 205). By means of this pastiche of death's time and life's as well as the correlates, he advertizes a cultured sensibility that consciously employs its learning to demonstrate its rich endowment of cultivated forms and its intelligence to shape and direct its existence.

All this self-promotion does not add up, however, to a vain, self-indulgent art. Both Skipper as the narrator and Hawkes' imagination are, without a doubt, cynosures. But at the same time they dedicate themselves to "saving" and being "saved"(e.g., 187). Hawkes does not intend by that word to save life from itself but rather to save it, economically and spiritually, by enhancement. Accordingly, his allusions and contrivance do not attach him nostalgically or desperately to a beautiful old order. He does not employ them, as say, T. S. Eliot did, to retreat into history, tradition, or conventional modes as a defense against the intolerable present. Instead, via them, while he performs the self-definition and self-affirmation to which his self-centered art is ineluctably devoted, he renders and celebrates that most fantastic kind of change, life's phoenix-like feat of redeeming itself out of its own death. The correlates and artifice, then, simply confirm and strengthen the commitment to life very evident thematically in the book.

Hawkes incisively perceived that such a salvation depended upon his obviating what Skipper calls "a broadside collision against Crooked Finger Rock"(187). He also recognized with equal astuteness that to avoid a disastrous collision his art would have to realize, as imaged in his figure of a blackbird sitting on a cow's rump, "the perfect union, the meeting of the fabulous herald and the life source"(101). He admits by leading into the phrase ending "Crooked Finger Rock" with "at least something, I thought, had saved us from a broadside collision" that such a perfect union is not easily attained, that salvation still in our time comes in mysterious ways.

The difficulty with which it comes and how it does so is illustrated by the ordeal of Skipper, a would-be savior by innate inclination but a blunderer in his efforts until he grows wise. Before that he sought wrongly to ward off harm from children and to save those who had no desire to be saved, the lovers of death like his mortician father, who commits suicide. Distrustful of life, and especially disturbed by "hot rods," his naive efforts at playing savior—of commanding at sea and securing Cassandra with a restrictive, legally sanctioned position in the world—lead to his domination by Miranda, a careless, hard-drinking "block of flesh and bone"(59). (She drinks, as does Skipper while they live together, *Old Grand-Dad,* indicative that her life embodies the sterile unprogressive changes of the forever old that can do no more than wear out and destroy.) Under her influence he is mercilessly buffeted about by the impersonal sea and wind and swept by these elements to the extremities, where Captain Red and Jomo, the half-man, wield demonic control over him. During this phase of his life, he "had gone too far"(195) or to the "distant parts of my kingdom"(204). It is then, while seasickness plagued him and Cassandra learned to sail, that he runs the risk of a broadside collision.

Yet, making no more secret of it than anything else in *Second Skin*, Hawkes specifies the means by which the extremities are eluded, Miranda triumphed over, and life firmly implanted upon the land. It is the "artificial inseminator." And that is a technological instrument designed to facilitate generation—not to control life tyranically but to assist it along its way. Hence Hawkes' artifice and art, his correlates and construction, do not function as history or cosmic law but as technology; they provide the materials and instruments of his craft. True, they mediate and moderate, but they are no more the source of life—"the seeds of life"(167) which in themselves possess the power of generation—than they are a refuge from or against it. As technological instruments, Hawkes is not bound by their set forms but can play fast and loose with them, as indeed he does by working his ironic twists upon, for example, metamorphosis and the Romantic, thereby bending them to human or living purposes rather than breaking life and man to conform to them.

Still, technology in itself, Hawkes realizes, can serve evil as well as good purposes. Which it does in Captain Red's boat, Jomo's artificial hand, and the hot rods of Jomo and Miranda—or whenever it is at the disposal of the "poor" in spirit. As a mediator and moderator, it places a bumper between colliding forces, but it does not endow with good life, and so it cannot by itself save. What saves Skipper and Hawkes' art is the "capacity for love" (2). That capacity emerges to the face when the fear of life and sexuality, its potent assertion, is replaced by the acceptance of it with the recognition that "virtue is everywhere"(98). Given the talent for it—which is purely a gift, and Hawkes obviously has been granted it—once the deadening anxieties are sloughed off, the radiant "virtue of life itself"(99) flows strong and steadily. That, "the life source," is the matrix of Hawkes' fabulous art.

Skipper exemplifies more specifically what the virtue of life entails when he triumphs over Miranda. He does not destroy her or even save Cassandra from her. He saves himself only. And he does that simply by turning his back and walking away, not by destroying death or the extremities, as it were, but by burying the dead seed of Cassandra's fetus and letting go, by abandoning Miranda and going on beyond her to something else, Catalina Kate, a woman of primitive vitality and vigor who prefers to live. With her he learns the final lesson of his futility in trying to defend others from their life when he fails to lift the iguana from Kate's back. This attempt does harm rather than good; it results in the iguana's defensive claws rending Kate's flesh, while when left alone it moves off of its own natural tendency. His triumph consists, then, of simply letting life have its way with him rather than desperately fighting it in the hopes of gaining absolute control over it. Once free of his frantic urge to frustrate death—or to possess an explanation of causality in order to impose a mechanistic frame upon life so that it might be controlled by force of will—he gives himself over to helping it joyously reach its proper ends, the creation of further life, by begetting a child and breeding, via his benign control, his herd of cows. Thus he triumphs not in the sense of dominating but by getting out from under Miranda's domination of him. He eludes her when he admits that he cannot forcefully save people but can only entice them by his vigor and charm. Thereafter he wins them with his relaxed and generous vitality, by loving coolly and freely rather than clasping in fearful anxiety.

When he leaves Miranda behind, Skipper automatically assumes his "new profession"(47) as an artificial inseminator, and then, in what is his maturity, letting life be, he becomes Hawkes' vehicle for professing the new. The benign life, healthy sexuality, and generous creativity of Skipper at this point and of Hawkes' art in *Second Skin* is especially evident in Skipper's final success at the cemetery on the Night of All Saints. He goes there, in effect, to baptize Catalina Kate's newly born baby—to perform a mass of sorts, including a feast of "Thick bread. Blackblood sausage. White wine"(209), whereby a definitive spirit will inhabit the baby's body. Skipper intercedes in the transaction and factilitates it with the artistry of his candles, which first produce an "artificial day"(208) when, carefully arranged on an old grave, they are "gems of the crude diadem" and "little flames popping up"(209). He induces the unknown soul from that grave to light up the smiles of himself and Kate and assume a reincarnation in the baby, who "look like the fella in the grave"(209) and Skipper pronounces "Light as a feather"(209). Through the agency of his art, Skipper unites old death with new flesh just as the moon is about "to suck the last light of our candles into the new day"(209). On this occasion his technology lends sharper focus and greater strength to the virtues of life inherent in "unruly nature"(187).

To this end—the miraculous incarnation of spirit in body—Hawkes devotes his living art. Tapping the life source, as a fabulous herald he joins the insubstantial with the substantial, transmits the abstract into the concrete. Under life's aegis, dead form in his hands metamorphoses into living form. In a sense his heraldry is indeed fabulous: it announces through a work purely of the imagination a truth knowable only through "myth" and "legend," that is, art. But in all other respects it is fabulous only ironically. It does not proclaim an other worldly supernatural revelation. Rather, as Skipper thrives on the "exhilarating images of my present life"(48), and others in his narrative thrive on his life present and presented, so Hawkes' fabulous heraldry presents life. Not an escape into fantasy but an articulation and admiration of life's truly fabulous power for saving itself, he lovingly exalts its capacity to be light, open, and full; luxuriant, simple, and comic; without underlying demons, ominous shadows, or hidden malices; a various, beautiful, bountiful, coruscating phenomenon. Because he so loves life, the supreme heraldic revelation of *Second Skin* is its illustration, by what it is, of the proper relation between art and life. In a living art and for a loving art of life, a vital and vigorous bond between energy and form is the proper good of the imagination. And that relation is specifically, "The sun in the evening. The moon at dawn. The still voice."(210)–three discreet entities and moments, two of them, ironic composites representative of nature's cyclical movement, providing the source of and being mediated by the serene, confident voice speaking evermore out of the stillness where sun evolves into night and moon evolves into day.

Stephen G. Nichols, Jr.

Vision and Tradition in *Second Skin*

"A kind of excellent dumb discourse"

The Tempest

A shaggy sea-wet islet pauses tideless
Under two hawks hovering. A dim
Washed heaven blue surmounts the wordless
Morning, its weighty world-wide asking trimmed
Down to summer silence. Was paradise
Like this before the need arose for it,
Before God made the book that broke the silence?

Man-made, the book was God. At his arising .
A thud of grim intelligence slammed shut
The summer silence. Up rose the wordy islet,
Awash with seas' fist rocky stutterings.
One man, one hut: an aleph-beth was started
With handy Adam to belie it, mouthing
How Eve most mothers summer's green abiding.

"Jawing of Genesis"

The first poem in Edwin Honig's *Gazabos*[1] is an appropriate point of departure for an essay on *Second Skin* for several reasons. Not only did Hawkes dedicate the novel to Honig and his wife, he has also acknowledged the impression made by this poem, and at least one other, "Island Storm," on

Stephen G. Nichols, Jr. is chairman of the department of comparative literature at Dartmouth College.
[1]New York: Clarke and Way, 1959, p. 3.

the long and complex genesis of the novel.[2] The poems are important for
what they can tell us of the subtle but persistent role of literary allusion—a
word almost too strong for the phenomenon we are dealing with in Hawkes'
work; literary *infusion* might be more appropriate—in the Hawkesian creative
process. Two themes of paramount importance to *Second Skin* are broached
in "Jawing of Genesis" and "Island Storm": the identification of island
worlds with pre-fall paradise and the post-fall infernal world, and the
recognition that the written word at once creates man's awareness of paradise
and imparts the grim intelligence of its loss. "Island Storm" adds to these
themes the image of the destruction of the world by flood:

> On such a day prophets used
> To rave about—"Stiff-necked mankind, remember
> Sodom and God's frown!" Through miles
> Of tensing acreage only two eyes peeped when it
> Came down. The road became a falls
> Where hubbubs fell to foam across a glazed surrendering
> Of channelled stone. In the hollow beat
> Of some annihilating warmth, tumorous old stumps
> Were ground to muck.   (11. 8-16)

as well as the correlative idea of the island as Ark in which one can survive the
holocaust if one can only hang on long enough:

> When at last the silence trickled in, I found
> The fungi like great plastered wounds,
> The stupefying sweetness everywhere. And when
> The weather turned gigantically
> And padded off, I found the world it left nearby:
> On the bloated attic floor
> Two drowned mice; through the skylight, one fir
> Permanently bowed; above the flooded
> Garden, the first fierce dart of an exploratory crow.
>   (11. 24-32)

These two poems, and others in the collection, present a dual concept of
island, as actuality and as archetype. They project that primordial emotion
aroused in us by the island image which has been so well described by Harold
C. Goddard in his essay on Shakespeare's *The Tempest,* a play very much a
part of the literary infusion in *Second Skin*:

An island is a bit of a higher element rising out of a lower—like a fragment
of consciousness thrusting up out of the ocean of unconsciousness. Like a
clearing in the wilderness or a walled city, like a temple or a monastery, it

[2]In private conversation and classroom discussion at Dartmouth College, January, 1970.

is a piece of cosmos set over against chaos and ready to defend itself if chaos, as it will be bound to do, tries to bring it back under its old domination. It is a magic circle, a small area of perfection shutting out all the rest of infinite space. What wonder then that an island has come to be the symbol of birth and rebirth, or that from the fabled Atlantis and that earthly island, the Garden of Eden, to the latest Utopia, an island, literal or metaphorical, is more often than any other the spot that the human imagination chooses for a fresh experiment in life.[3]

In talking about the genesis of *Second Skin*, Hawkes makes no secret of the fact that he had always wanted to write a novel about an island, and that when he first saw Vinalhaven (the actual island in Penobscot Bay, Maine, of Honig's poems and the first part of *Second Skin*), he knew he had found his island. The first attempt to write about Vinalhaven, however, resulted in a short story, "The Nearest Cemetery" (1963), recently re-issued in *Lunar Landscapes*.[4] While "The Nearest Cemetery" certainly has some of the flavor of "The Gentle Island" sequence of *Second Skin*—although little of its dark humor and stark tragedy—it does not possess the thematic resonances of the novel, particularly as regards the duality of the island as at once real and archetypal. For although the short story does adumbrate the theme of two islands, Bloody Clamshell and the state prision,[5] including the narrator's journey from one to the other, it does not cast these islands as polar opposites, one an infernal world presided over by a female devil, the other, a paradisal world ruled by a benevolent, loving Ariel *cum* Pan. The Barber's motivation for telling his story in "The Nearest Cemetery," like Skipper's in *Second Skin*, springs from his desire to communicate his victory over his rivals, but the triumph is a negative one—the murder of the woman they all love—and the world of the prison island as starkly infernal and sterile as that of Bloody Clam.

Similarly, "The Nearest Cemetery" shares *Second Skin*'s preoccupation with death, but the Barber can never boast with Skipper that he has finished with death, nor does the story assert the theme of birth and rebirth (the "Second Skin" theme) as the ultimate triumph over death. Between the writing of "The Nearest Cemetery" and the creation of the novel, the idea of island as archetype slowly matured in the author's mind until it attained at least as strong a hold as the image of the island as actuality, the dimension

---

[3] *The Meaning of Shakespeare* (Chicago: University of Chicago Press, 1951), II, 287.
[4] New York: New Directions, 1969, pp. 43-50.
[5] "Like an island. In the first sunset that prison was an island without rock or spume or salt, an island without buried barns and sea air pollinated apples that fall from fractured boughs to rot on the shore line with periwinkles—island almost the size of Bloody Clam but with gongs and siren instead of buoys and twenty-eight miles inland from the sea. So that day I only went from one island, Bloody Clam, to another island lying in a white valley across which move not boats, orange and black, but a few muddy dump trucks and, occasionally, the Marshal's car." (*Ibid.*, p. 45.)

presented in the short story. Just as his visits to Vinalhaven occasioned an imaginative revery on the stark, North Atlantic island as archetype of an infernal world, so the setting in which *Second Skin* was actually composed—a tropical island in the Lesser Antilles—touched off a similar revery on the tropical island as the archetypal earthly paradise in the sense captured in the Goddard quotation above. In each case, the actuality of the author's visits to the islands, while important in terms of the immediate impact on his imagination, is of much less significance than his imaginative vision of them which, by his own testimony, antedates the actual experiences by many years and, in fact, prompted them. That imaginative vision, uniquely Hawkesian as it is, nonetheless, and as the evidence of the Honig poems suggests, derives from a real and subtle interaction between private vision and literary tradition.

For Hawkes' novels are at once refreshingly *sui generis,* original in the best sense of the word, and yet selfconsciously reflective of kinds of literature one has read previously. *The Lime Twig* is certainly not a detective story as that genre comes from the pen of Agatha Christie, Michael Innes or Dorothy Sayers. Nevertheless, as the title and the names of the principal protagonists, Michael Banks[6] and his wife, indicate, it does fit most of the definitions by which that genre is generally identified, especially as concerns the dialectic of innocence and guilt. By the same token, *The Beetle Leg* does not fit the obvious cliché of the drugstore western, but it did grow out of a revery inspired by a pair of second-hand cowboy boots acquired in Montana[7] and it does recapture in its own way the qualities of land and people which sectional writers as diverse as Steinbeck, Faulkner, and Zane Grey have tried to portray.[8]

The literary resonances emanating from *Second Skin,* however, are of quite a different kind from the generic or stylistic resemblances found in Hawkes' earlier works. In *Second Skin,* the whole cultural tradition of Western literature, from Greek myths to contemporary poetry, serves as background material on which Hawkes draws in an eclectic, but persistent fashion. These references may function in a fairly straightforward manner to provide contrasting comparisons between characters in *Second Skin* and well-known

---

[6]Michael Banks' name is deliberately lifted from *Mary Poppins* to underline the innocence of the chief victims. The innocence is, nevertheless, combined with complicity, for Hawkes feels that the Bankses, like Hencher and Skipper, are accomplices to as well as victims of the evil they portray. See "John Hawkes: an Interview," *Wisconsin Studies in Contemporary Literature,* VI (1965), 151-152, 154-155.

[7]From a classroom discussion at Dartmouth College, January 13, 1970.

[8]As always in a Hawkes novel, the feeling for the setting is most strikingly rendered in terms of the characters; indeed one might well speak of a symbiotic relationship between characters and the objects on their landscapes: characters are portrayed by association with objects—objects which take on a kind of personality like Ma Lampson's deep dish skillet or the sheriff's jail, or the dam itself.

mythical or literary antecedents. Thus Cassandra who, unlike her namesake does not predict doom but rather, pale and listless Helen that she is, precipitates it. Or Miranda, more obviously a Sycorax—even to the clouds of greasy smoke fuming from the saucers of asthma powder—than the ingenue of Shakespeare's play, even though Skipper, like the reader, is at first tempted to make the rapprochement between Shakespeare's innocent heroine and her cynical and disillusioned namesake:

> After Fernandez there was Miranda. I hear that name—Miranda, Miranda! —and once again quicken to its false suggestiveness, feel its rhapsody of sound, the several throbs of the vowels, the very music of charity, innocence, obedience, love. For a moment I seem to see both magic island and imaginary girl. But Miranda was the widow's name—out of what perversity, what improbable desire I am at a loss to say—and no one could have given a more ugly denial to that heartbreaking and softly fluted name than the tall and treacherous woman. Miranda. The widow. . . . Raw-boned and handsome woman, unconventional and persistent widow, old antagonist on a black Atlantic island, there she was—my mon-ster, my Miranda, final challenge of our sad society and worthy of all the temperance and courage I could muster. Now I think of her as my black butterfly. And now—obviously—the scars are sweet.(5)[9]

Paris, Clytemnestra, Iphigenia, Cleopatra, Ariel, all figure in the system of eponymous metaphors used by Hawkes not only to give his characters contrastive nuances of various kinds, but also to imbue them with that classical timelessness—consisting of a simultaneous and paradoxical remote-ness and immediacy—that looms so large in the work. The main character and narrator, Skipper, is the person most liberally endowed with literary eponyms. "Naming Names," appropriately enough the first chapter, allows him to present himself as a kind of mythical figure, a character brushed with the supernatural and androgynous qualities of a Prospero, an Ariel or even, in a more heroic vein, a Ulysses:

> Had I been born my mother's daughter instead of son . . . I would not have matured into a muscular and self-willed Clytemnestra but rather into a large and innocent Iphigenia betrayed on the beach. A large and slow-eyed and smiling Iphigenia, to be sure, even more full to the knife than that real girl struck down once on the actual shore. (1-2)

> With Hamlet I should say that once, not long ago, I became my own granddaughter's father, giving her the warmth of my two arms and generous smile, substituting for each drop of the widow's poison the milk of my courageous heart. (2)

---

[9] *Second Skin* (New York: New Directions, 1964). Page references to *Second Skin* will be cited in parentheses following each quotation.

Here it is, the declaration of faith which I say aloud to myself when I
pause and prop my feet on the window sill where the hummingbird is
destroying his little body and heart and eye among the bright vines and
stick flowers and leaves: *I have soon to journey to a lonely island in a
distant part of my kingdom. But I shall return before the winter storms
begin.* Prince Paris, *I leave my wife, Helen, in your care. Guard her well.
See that no harm befalls her.* (45-46)

I was tossed up spent and half-naked on the invisible shore of our
wandering island—old Ariel in sneakers, sprite surviving in bald-headed
man of fair complexion. . . . (162)

Important as the eponymous metaphors are to the novel, they are but a
part of the larger system of literary allusion helping to determine the
structure of *Second Skin.* Hawkes has said that his novels are "structured"
rather than "plotted"[10] so it is not surprising to find an ingenious use of
thematic allusion as a key principle behind the book's structure. Both the
verbal and psychological coherence of the work depend greatly upon the
systematic exploitation of such themes as those broached in Honig's poems or
in works of a more widespread cultural diffusion like the *Odyssey, The
Tempest, The Divine Comedy, Ulysses.* Such works postulate life in terms of
a movement between two worlds—often metaphorically or literally identified
with islands—one of which is ruled by death, violence, war, brutality, and
hatred, while the other realizes within itself—as defense against the other—all
the opposite potential: life, love, peace, grace, courage and creation. The
hero's task is to develop the positive potential of the latter world in the face
of the threats offered by the cesspool of negative potential represented by the
former. More simply, he must reach the paradisal world by risking the dangers
of the infernal one. When Hawkes says that Skipper is "ultimately a figure of
responsibility, indeed the very essence of the responsible individual,"[11] he
can do so authoritatively knowing that Skipper—who appears at first blush to
be a good example of the modern anti-hero—belongs to the tradition of
driven heroes from classical times to the present who move through the
nightmare of death and violence to reach their "floating island," their
"wandering island" redolent of the fragrance of lime and golden under the
wheel of its hot sun.

Traditionally, however, plot and narrative focus upon the reality of the

10 "My novels are not highly plotted, but certainly they're elaborately structured. I
began to write fiction on the assumption that the true enemies of the novel were plot,
character, setting, and theme, and having once abandoned these familiar ways of
thinking about fiction, totality of vision or structure was really all that remained. And
structure—verbal and psychological coherence—is still my largest concern as a writer.
Related or corresponding event, recurring image and recurring action, these constitute
the essential substance or meaningful density of my writing. However, as I suggested
before, this kind of structure can't be planned in advance but can only be discovered in
the writing process itself." ("John Hawkes: An Interview," p. 149.)
11 From a private conversation, January 12, 1970.

journey between the two worlds. The story opens, in most cases, before the goal has been reached and ranges back over the preceding events as the hero moves closer to his goal. With the attainment of that goal, the work ends. In Skipper's case, Hawkes has chosen to place the emphasis not upon the journey as fact, as actuality, but upon the journey as vision, as a recreation by the narrator of his previous existence as a necessary precondition to understanding his present.

It is important to underline the quality of the journey as vision because Hawkes' narrative is so vivid that the reader frequently finds himself caught up in the actuality of the journey, forgetting that it is in fact a recollection, with all the intensity and selectivity associated with dream vision. For one thing, many, if not most of the scenes from the infernal world part of the book take place at night or in the early morning, pre-dawn hours. In this otherworld atmosphere of darkness and uncertain light, the actions take on a weird grotesqueness which lends them portentousness in the same way the system of eponyms give depth to the characters. Scenes like the tattooing parlor, the bus wreck, the night of the high school dance, the drag race in Cleopatra's car, the scene of Fernandez' murder, the mutiny on the *U.S.S. Starfish*—even the voyage of the *Peter Poor,* which takes place in the daytime, has a nightmare quality which tends to make us associate it with darkness—all these bear distinct reminiscences of literary evocations of the underworld, especially of such modern classics as Leopold Bloom in Nighttown, or the narrator of Céline's *Journey to the End of the Night,* Ferdinand Bardamu, who gradually loses himself in darkness.[12] The purpose of this observation is less to postulate literary analogues than to explain the quality of vision, as opposed to realism, which resonate from such key scenes in *Second Skin.* To take but one example, the bus wreck *qua* shipwreck in which realism and surrealism, actuality and fantasy inextricably intermingle in a manner only possible when the bounds between the imaginative world and the outer world have been dissolved by the visionary eye. Temporal perspective is confused, and space becomes the inner space of emotional perception, defying the orderly laws of the physicist by which we ordinarily define the relationship of objects in space and time:

> But I must have lain there musing and grumbling for hours, for several hours at least, before the tire exploded.
> "Oh!" came Cassandra's whispered shriek, her call for help, and I pinioned Pixie's rump, I sank down, my knees were heaved into flight, Cassandra was floating, reaching out helplessly for her child. In the next instant the rear half of the bus was off the road and sailing out, I could feel, in a seventy-eight-mile-an-hour dive into the thick of the night. Air

---

[12] Hawkes makes no secret of his admiration for Céline, particularly *Voyage au bout de la nuit.* It is perhaps the modern European novel he has most appreciated from a professional viewpoint. See "John Hawkes: An Interview," p. 141.

brakes in full emergency operation. Accidental blow to the horn followed
by ghastly and idiotic trill on the trumpet. Driving rear end of the bus
beginning to describe an enormous arc—fluid blue path of greatest
destruction—and forward portion lurching, hammering, banging driver's
black head against invisible wall. Now, O Christopher . . . and then the
crash.

. . . And in this abrupt cessation of our sentimental journey, becoming
aware of moonlight in the window and of the thin black line of the empty
highway stretching away out there. . . . The bus was a dark blue dusty
shadow, deceptive wreck; our skid-marks were long black treacherous
curves in the desert; the highway was a dead snake in the distance; the
wind was strong. We stood there with the unfamiliar desert beneath our
feet, stood with our heads thrown back to the open night sky which was
filled with tiny brief threads of performing meteors. . . . Then in our
roller-skating stance—hand to elbow, hand to waist—we began to move
together, to stagger together in the moonlight, and over my shoulder and
flung to either side of the harsh black visible track of our flight from the
road I saw the prostrate silhouettes of a dozen fat giant cacti that had
been struck head on by the bus and sent sailing. For a moment I saw
them, these bloated shapes of scattered tackling dummies that marked the
long wild curve of our reckless detour into the dark and milky night.
Abandoned. As we were abandoned.

. . . While the black-faced driver hauls out his hydraulic jack and drags it
toward the mutilated tire which has come to rest in a natural rock garden
of crimson desert flowers and tiny bulbs and a tangle of prickly parasitic
leaves. All crushed to a pulp. Mere pustules beneath that ruined tire.

It was the dead center of some nightmare accident but here at least,
crouching and squatting together in the lee of the bus, there was no wind.
Only the empty windows, shadows, scorched point of the crippled
monster . . .and the driver—puttees, goggles, snappy cap and movements
of ex-fighter-pilot, fierce nigger carefully trained by the Greyhound
line—bustled about the enormous sulphuric round of the tire. Refusing
assistance, removing peak-shouldered military jacket, retaining cap,
strutting in riding britches, fingering the jack, clucking at long rubber
ribbons of the burst tire: "Why don't you fellows sing a little and pass the
time?" But only more performing meteors and this hell's nigger greasing
both arms and whistling, tossing high into the air his bright wrenches.
(34-37)

The demonic quality of the scene derives largely from the rhetorical
transformation of a fairly banal incident, when viewed dispassionately, into
an emotionally-charged, even surrealistic tableau conjured up before our eyes,
as it were, by Skipper's visionary prowess.[13] As is so often the case in
Hawkes' work, the setting or narrative incident serves as an object of

---

[13]Such passages of almost poetic rhetoric illustrate perfectly what Hawkes has called
"the saving beauties of language" ("Interview," p. 144). They have the same quality of
showmanship—in terms of Skipper's authorial persona—revealed by Prospero when he
says:

imaginative revery for the narrator, just as Hawkes himself lets his imagination play upon the actuality of his island visits until they are gradually interiorized and transformed. Setting and incident are engulfed by the narrator's consciousness and translated into the subjective, visionary idiom used by Hawkes' protagonists to construct the lunar landscapes they interpose between themselves and the world. This interaction between Skipper and the objects he perceives, decomposes and recomposes in his mind is characteristic of Hawkes' narrative style, accounting for the dreamlike quality of much of his work. We are rarely able to distinguish flatly between the interior world composed in the mind of a Hawkes' protagonist and the world in which he functions, for the one defines and circumscribes the other.[14]

The narrator's mind may even dominate perfectly realistic-seeming scenes by "freezing" them in mid-motion, much as Seurat sought to do with his technique of *pointilisme*.[15] These pieces of description, suspending motion

---

> I must
> Bestow upon the eyes of this young couple
> Some vanity of mine art: it is my promise.
> And they expect it from me. (*The Tempest*, IV, i)

[14] The setting of any given scene in Hawkes' novels will almost invariably figure prominently in the character development achieved in the scene. Rarely will a setting remain unchanged from one end of the scene to another. Changes in the perspective of the setting are often used to signal changes in character, as though the total action depended upon a constant metamorphosis of the reader's and character's perspective. For example, in "A Little Bit of the Old Slap and Tickle" (*Lunar Landscapes*, pp. 26-27), Hawkes evokes the graveyard of abandoned warships as part of the panorama unfolding below Sparrow when he appears on the edge of the cliff. At first mention, nothing distinguishes the ship graveyard; but it is mentioned three times in rapid succession, each time in a way that brings it closer to Sparrow's own existence—as though man and rusty metal were advancing to meet one another—until finally it becomes a metaphor for his slightly surrealistic domestic world (sharply distinguished from "the world from which he had come"). By the end of the story, Sparrow and his wife, especially his wife, have become inextricably interwoven with the rusting hulks: each explains and identifies the other.

[15] The falling bomber witnessed by Hencher at the beginning of *The Lime Twig* is a marvelous example of frozen motion:

Large, brown, a lifeless airplane returning, it was one of our own and I saw it suddenly approach out of the snow perhaps a hundred feet above the garret and slow as a child's kite. Big and blackish-brown with streaks of ice across the nose, which was beginning to rise while the tail sank behind in the snow, it was simply there, enormous and without a trace of smoke, the engines dead and one aileron flapping in the wind. And ceasing to climb, ceasing to move, a vast and ugly shape stalled against the snow up there, the nose dropped and beneath the pilot's window I saw the figure of a naked woman painted against the bomber's pebbly surface. Her face was snow, something back of her thigh had sprung a leak and the thigh was sunk in oil. But her hair, her long white head of hair was shrieking in the wind as if the inboard engine was sucking the strands of it.

Her name was Reggie's Rose and she was sitting on the black pack of a parachute. Dipped, shuddered, banged up and down for a moment—I could see the lifted rudder then, swinging to and fro above the tubular narrowing of its fuselage—and during that slapping glide the thick wings did not fall, no frenzied hand wiped the pilot's icy windscreen, no tiny torch switched on to prove this final and outrageous landfall. ([New York, New Directions, 1961], p. 19.)

and time, stand out in bold relief from the surrounding narrative; often coming at moments of stress, they reveal the anxious sensitivity felt by the narrators, particularly Skipper and his prototype, Hencher, for expressions of threat or hostility:

> And the two of them, widow in black, Captain Red in black double-breasted suit, swung out to the middle of the floor, towered above that handful of undernourished high school girls and retarded boys. *Two tall black figures locked length to length, two faces convulsed in passion, one as long and white and bony as a white mare's face, the other crimson, leathery, serrated like the bald head to which it belonged, and the young boys and girls making way for them, scattering in the path of their slow motion smoke, staring up at them in envy, fear, shocked surprise.*(80, my italics)

Such passages of frozen motion are also typical of the dream mechanism, freed as they are from the ordinary laws of space and time. They are but one more reminder that the book is conceived as a long revery, a retrospective reflection undertaken for compelling psychological reasons:

> Highlights of helplessness? Mere trivial record of collapse? Say, rather, that it is the chronicle of recovery, the history of courage, the dead reckoning of my romance, the act of memory, the dance of shadows. And all the earmarks of pageantry, if you will, the glow of Skipper's serpentine tale. (162)

Vision or actuality, the evocation of his past does represent a risk, just as surely as if Skipper were to plunge himself once again into the horrors he recollects. For despite his protestations, Skipper is indulging less in a cockcrow of triumph, than in an act of ritual exorcism, a recreation of himself as he was, prisoner and accomplice of death, in order to reveal the full extent of his rebirth, his new-found wholeness and success. But as he recreates his past, he knows he will be seen as he was by the reader as well as himself; hence his anxiety to assert the transient nature of that previous being, or rather to stress the positive qualities of grace, courage, self-sacrifice which brought him through the dangerous voyage. It is for these reasons that he has recourse to the eponymous metaphors discussed earlier, or the traditional infernal-paradisal world polar structure for his narrative. For within the expectations of the theme, Skipper's role as hero and ultimate victor over his enemies will be assured.

In the tradition of modern fiction, *Second Skin* deals with the discovery of the self by the self—which is one reason, perhaps, why it is Hawkes' only novel narrated entirely in the first person. From this perspective, we see that the infernal world recreated by Skipper is a world made so less by the brutality of the Tremlows, Jomos, Fernandez, Captain Reds, Bubs, and Mirandas than by the shock of having to recognize and portray for us the extent of his own complicity in that brutality, that lust for death and violence:

> So I played for him, played Brahms while my father must have been loading the pistol . . . I played with no thought of him, really, but he must have gagged a little to himself in there, choked like a man coughing up blood for the first time as he tried to decide how best to use the nickel-plated weapon, forced his fingers inside the trigger guard . . . So I played on, phantom accomplice to his brutal act, and all the while hoping, I think, for success and pleased with the song. (160)

> But if my own poor father was Death himself, as I think he was, then certainly I was right to tell Cassandra how familiar I was with the seeds of death. Wasn't I myself, as a matter of fact, simply that? Simply one of those little black seeds of death? (161)

> And the dawn was lying out there and bleeding to death while I fidgeted outside Cassandra's door—accomplice, father, friend, traveling companion, yes, old chaperone, but lover and destroyer too . . . (175-176)

The dividing line between the two worlds is thus not spatial or temporal (they are both contained simultaneously within Skipper's mind) so much as psychological. "The Gentle Island," the name only semi-ironically applied to the infernal world of the first island,[16] is a world in which Skipper discovers his self divided against itself. Skipper's image of himself as a whole being, full of love and loved in return—the hero who effectively creates his world through love and courage, freed from anxiety and pure of brutality—this image he shows to be repeatedly shattered in the infernal world, challenged by those very beings to whose violence he has been an accomplice; indeed, whose violence one might say he has created, or at least recreated, as author of what he repeatedly calls "my naked history."

> And then she looked at me and slowly, calmly whispered, "Nobody wants to kiss you, Skipper." (43)

---

[16] "The Gentle Island" obviously has ironic overtones as a title, but, from Skipper's viewpoint, gentleness becomes a defense against the brutality of the island. The cliché homily satirically glued to the bathroom mirror in Miranda's house:

> Wake with a Loving Thought
> Work with a Happy Thought
> Sleep with a Gentle Thought

is taken seriously by Skipper: "Sleep with a gentle thought, I remembered, and did my best" (97). Skipper's humor redeems the cliché in a manner calculated not to endear him to Miranda.

I heard the gasping breaths below turn to laughter and for a long while hesitated to enter my icy room. Because of the dressmaker's dummy. Because . . . she had placed this dummy at the head of my bed and dressed it in my naval uniform so that the artificial bosom swelled my white tunic and the artificial pregnancy of the padded belly puffed out the broad front of my official white duck pants which she had pinned to the dummy with a pair of giant safety pins rammed through the felt. Cuffs of the empty sleeves thrust in the pockets, white hat cocked outrageously on the wire head—desperate slant of the black visor, screaming angle of the golden bird—oh, it was a jaunty sight she had prepared for me. But of course I ignored it as best I could, tried to overlook the fresh dark gouts of ketchup she had flung down the front of that defiled figure, and merely shut my door, at least spared my poor daughter from having to grapple with that hapless effigy of my disfigured self. (67)

But in the rusty disreputable interior of that frozen junk heap she had mocked me with the beauty of her naked stern, had challenged, aroused, offended me with the blank wall of nudity, and I perceived a cruel motive somewhere. (96)

That's all you are, Papa Cue Ball. The father of a woman who produces a premature child. The husband of a woman who kills herself. I renounce it, Papa Cue Ball. I renounce this family, I renounce this kind of a man. (129)

Knocked down my guard and socked me in the mouth, and I should have ducked at least because the line of the blow was as clear as the hate in the steady eyes . . . "Wait," I said, and my mouth was bleeding, "wait a minute . . . you don't know what you're doing . . . you'll be sorry, Tremlow."
    But he hit me in the mouth again. Same fist, same mouth, more bloody mud, more pain. Why not the nose, I thought, or the naked eye, or the stomach, why this furious interest in my loose and softspoken mouth? (146)

Other examples of the brutality directed at Skipper and his image might be cited, but the above should be ample to demonstrate the thoroughness and intensity of Skipper's recreation of these moments of self-degradation. For something in Skipper always stops him from responding to the assaults in a manner that might redeem his image in a conventionally heroic manner. Rather than meeting force with force, he meets it with acquiescence, complicity. He refuses to permit Sonny to fell Tremlow, the leader of the *Starfish* mutiny, with an axe, and subsequently will not order the crew to fire upon the fleeing boats of the mutineers. He is thus at once victim and accomplice of the mutiny, a brutal act which will be eclipsed only by the treachery of Captain Red, Jomo, and Cassandra's death.

Similarly, aboard the fateful voyage of the *Peter Poor,* Skipper has the lucidity to understand that Bub has hit him with the tire iron and will hit him again; a plan of action even flashes through his mind, but he passively submits to the second assault, knowing as he does so that Red and Jomo will profit from his unconsciousness to complete their conquest of Cassandra. Skipper thus recognizes his complicity in his daughter's destruction, a process begun when he urged her disastrous marriage to Fernandez.

In the light of this persistent brutalizing of his self-image (a process made bearable for the reader by the brilliant flashes of humor which accompany the ridicule), Skipper's visionary recreation of his journey proves him to be the man of courage he claims to be. By forcing himself to relive so vividly those moments of supreme degradation, Skipper runs the real risk of losing faith in the image of himself that has sustained him through the actual indignities—which at the time he was too busy living through to observe with the detachment made possible by their recreation—and of finally acquiescing to the counter image set forth so plausibly by the Circes and Polyphemuses that people the world he creates. Like many of his literary antecedents, Skipper knows that true adversity lies not in physical suffering, but in the mental anguish, the anxiety which accompanies the threatened annihilation of self-identity: the will to believe that one is at least in part the person one believes oneself to be.

Since he cannot meet force with force, the traditional recourse of the epic hero, Skipper meets this threat in the most effective way he can: by turning to the word that controls the action. In the Homeric sense, he becomes not a doer of deeds, but a sayer of words, the author of his naked history. In this capacity, even the act of portraying his self-degradation as thoroughly as he does becomes an affirmation of his new being, a being dedicated to creation. In a real sense, Skipper becomes a symbol of the artist-as-mortal, and his story, a biography of the making of the artist in the tradition made familiar by Joyce's Stephen Dedalus or Proust's young Marcel, who experience a certain abortive existence believing themselves to be feckless, ineffective and slightly ridiculous, only to emerge, ultimately, in a new form as authoritative and powerful masters of their own and others' destiny. They have learned the transforming power of the word, as the writers of *Genesis* understood that power, or as Honig conveyed it in the poems quoted earlier.

From the opening paragraph of *Second Skin,* it is clear that Skipper revels in his authorial persona, revels in it and handles it with sensitivity and skill. The figure of the lighthearted and ebullient lover of words is quite a different man indeed from the suffering victim, and yet the same quality of self-awareness pervades the two versions of self. For the authorial persona recognizes that from childhood on he has had a weakness for rhetoric and an apparently unfounded but unshakeable conviction that someday he would be able to make use of this talent:

For it is time now to recall that sad little prophetic passage from my
school boy's copybook with its boyish valor and its antiquity, and to
admit that the task of memory has only brightened these few brave
words, and to confess that even before my father's suicide and my
mother's death I always knew myself destined for this particular journey,
always knew this speech to be the one I would deliver from an empty
promontory or in an empty grove and to no audience, since of course
history is a dream already dreamt and destroyed. But now the passage,
the speech with its boyish cadences, flavor of morality, its soberness and
trust. . . . My confession? My declaration of heart and faith? "I have soon
to journey to a lonely island . . . guard her well . . ." Monstrous small
voice. Rhetorical gem. And yet it is the sum of my naked history, this
statement by a man of fancy, this impassioned statement of a man of
courage. I might have known from the copybook what I was destined for.
(45-46)

And so when he comes to fulfill his destiny and compose his naked history,
Skipper uses as the structure for this retrospective revery the two tangible
proofs that he has fulfilled his purpose and justified his self-faith: the child he
begets on Catalina Kate and the book he begets on himself. Seven years after
burying the fetus of Cassandra's last pathetic love—grotesque farewell present
from the black widow—and escaping from the infernal island, Skipper
conceives a child on Catalina Kate and begins his long-meditated confession:

So in six months and on the Night of All Saints Catalina Kate will bear
her child—our child—and I shall complete my history, my evocation
through a golden glass, my hymn to the invisible changing serpents of the
wind, complete this the confession of my triumph, this my diary of an
artificial inseminator. At the very moment Catalina Kate comes due my
crabbed handwriting shall explode in a concluding flourish, and I will be
satisfied. I will be fifty-nine years old and father to innumerable bright
living dreams and vanquished memories. (49)

Anthony C. Santore

Narrative Unreliability
and the Structure of *Second Skin*

> James gave us all the beauties, delicacies, psychic complications of a kind
> of bestial sensibility.
>
> John Hawkes[1]

Descriptions of the novels of John Hawkes stress innovation and invention, but in *Second Skin,* it is his use of a traditional literary device that provides the key to appreciating both the comedy and the suggestion of hope that Hawkes claims for the novel.[2] In making his narrator highly unreliable, Hawkes is solidly in a tradition that reaches back in American literature to Irving, Melville, Hawthorne, Poe, and Henry James. James, in particular, was very successful in his use of the unreliable narrator—*The Turn of the Screw,* "The Aspern Papers," and "The Author of Beltraffio" come most quickly to mind. Skipper, the narrator of *Second Skin,* embodies "all the beauties, delicacies, psychic complications of a kind of bestial sensibility" that Hawkes praised in James.

Skipper's unreliability as a narrator can be traced directly to his untruthfulness to himself, for it is only by suppressing the truth that he is able to endure his life and to bring order into it. This self-deception is the protective layer, the second skin, that Skipper uses to shield himself from all the unpleasant facts of his life. By distorting the truth of their existence or their meaning, he can excuse himself from responsibility for the pain he has caused and, at the end of the novel, he is at peace. Nearly every reviewer and critic has been successfully deceived by Skipper. T. A. Hanzo, for example, sees Skipper as "scapegoat and victim" rather than as the menace that he is to those around him; and W. M. Frohock is clearly aware of misinformation, but blames Hawkes instead of Skipper. Moreover, most of them comment critically on the confusion or pointlessness they find, but here, too, fail to hold the narrator responsible.[3] Skipper himself admits to being deceptive—at least to Cassandra, by "sparing her certain details, withholding others, failing

---

Anthony C. Santore teaches at Muhlenberg College.

[1] John Enck, "John Hawkes: An Interview," *WSCL,* VI (Summer 1965), 142.
[2] Enck, p. 146. See also John Graham, "John Hawkes on his Novels," *MR,* VII (1966), 459, where Hawkes describes the end of the novel as "affirmative," with the baby and the final scene representing "a sort of continuing life."
[3] T. A. Hanzo, "The Two Faces of Matt Donelson," *The Sewanee Review,* LXIII (Winter 1965), 111; W. M. Frohock, "John Hawkes' Vision of Violence," *Southwest Review,* L (Winter 1965), 72. See also Stanley Kauffmann, "Further Adventures of the Novel," *The New Republic,* CL (June 6, 1964), 22, who thinks the novel "seems to exist for the sake of its admittedly exceptional prose;" and Christopher Ricks, "Chamber of Horrors,"

somehow to convey the true tonality of the thing"(149)[4]–but he may not really be aware of how complete is his *self*-deception. He excuses himself, as far as his conscious deceptions are concerned, by calling them "the act of memory, the dance of shadows," and "Skipper's serpentine tale"(162).

Probably the most important element in the novel wherein the narrator is unreliable and self-deceptive is in relation to his courage and bravery. He refers to himself in these terms many times, and each time, ironically, it is his *weakness* that is apparent to the reader and is causing pain for others. Apart from several general references, there are specific references at moments when courage is really required, such as in the soldiers' scene when he refers to himself as a "solitary sentinel"(38) and tells Cassandra to be brave at least four times(42) while she is being raped—or, at the very least, molested. At the dance, he describes himself as "her guardian, her only defense"(81); yet he is powerless to stop anything, including the snowball attack and the molesting of Cassandara on the dance floor. When the iguana is atop Kate, he tells her to have courage, but closes his eyes because he cannot face it(106), just as he closes his eyes at several other moments of danger.

There are two other cowardly reactions to danger to which Skipper resorts. One is sleeping, as before the Tremlow attack(142), on Red's boat(186), and in the iguana scene(108). The other is his reaction after the danger has passed: he makes excuses for his not having acted. As Tremlow is escaping, he "should have unlimbered one of the three-inch guns and ordered them picked off"(148), but he does not; on Red's boat, "had it not been for Crooked Finger Rock [he] might have done something"(186) and after the iguana leaves, he "would have gone after him with a stone had it not been for the failing light and for Catalina Kate"(109).

Clearly, the position of Ship's Captain has connotations of power and authority like no other profession, but Skipper is not even manly enough to face tattooing without "terror"; and he had once been unable even to be tattooed with a "small initial M" for mother(17). The irony of the nickname "Skipper" is obvious. (The name of his ship, *Starfish,* is complementary irony

---

New Statesman, LXXI (March 11, 1966), 339-40, who thinks that the novel "has its failures, most obviously a dissipating fragmentariness."

Important exceptions are three critics who are aware that there is a problem with the narrator: Susan Sontag, in "A New Life for an Old One," *New York Times Book Review,* April 5, 1964, p. 5, calls the novel "*the apologia pro vita sua*" of the narrator; and Peter Brooks, in *Encounter,* XXVI (June 1966), 68-72, sees the "point of view" as "both unreliable and banal," and that Skipper writes this history "to prove that despite the series of 'brutal acts' to which he has been subjected, he is a man of both 'love and courage.' " See also John Kuehl's *Creative Writing & Rewriting* (New York, 1967), pp. 284-287, where he, in addition to seeing Skipper as "highly conscious of an audience" and *Second Skin* as "an explanation," presents several pages of penetrating commentary on several vital points. See also Graham, p. 459, where Hawkes explains that using the first-person narrator was a major consideration in writing the novel.

[4] John Hawkes, *Second Skin* (New York: New Directions, 1964). All references are to this edition.

because the starfish is as meek and inoffensive in its marine world as Skipper is in his. His other nickname, "Papa Cue Ball," also fits into the pattern, the cue ball being another blank, numberless, and isolated member of its society. Furthermore, the creature named "Edward" after him is a steer, an emasculated bull, who tries unsuccessfully to mount the fertile Phyllis. Skipper acknowledges their relationship, but unenthusiastically: "my name-sake—reluctantly I say that name, reluctantly admit that name"[168].) As a ship's captain, Skipper simply had not been effective; playing at religion with the chaplain, and reading and sleeping in the face of mutiny. The troublesome point is that he will not admit the truth even to himself. Why else does he not tell of Kate's pain with the iguana, but rather calls it "the dragon"(108) and the "succubus"(109) making his opponent supernatural and, incidentally, female? Furthermore, he reaches for it with his eyes closed, and describes *his* "agony" and not Kate's as he tries to pull it off. And why does he not tell of Cassandra's fate on Red's boat, or of Tremlow's sodomy, if it is not that he must deceive himself in order to make his present life with Kate and Sonny as peaceful as he needs it to be?

It is this self-deception that causes problems for the reader because it makes the narrative unreliable. The foundation of this self-deception is in Skipper's life-long refusal to acknowledge his impotence and possible homosexual inclinations.

A brief look at the structure of the novel will reveal how the truth is hidden, but discernible. Hawkes considers his novels "elaborately struc-tured,"[5] and *Second Skin* is that, being carefully woven of two threads: life before Sonny's island, and life on it. As Skipper unravels them, the two threads complement each other. As the events of the past life (or first skin) become more painful, those of the present (or second skin) become more joyous; as the idea of death in the old life becomes irresistibly stronger, the idea of life in the present becomes overpoweringly so; and as the old life ends with the death of a mother and her unborn fetus, the present ends with the birth of a healthy child to a healthy mother. Skipper emphasizes the more positive aspects of the present life by balancing them against the negative of the past. In the old life, attack after successful attack is made on Skipper's manhood, but in the new life, there are no attacks to prove his impotence. Skipper is the artificial inseminator—the artificiality being of no importance, the capacity for insemination all-important. He is now happy, productive, and life-giving.

On the other hand, every episode of personal interrelationship in the past life seems to emphasize his impotence and the resulting pain to himself and to those around him. Skipper's relationship with his parents may be the psychological basis for his problem. In the first pages of the novel, he says, "Had I been my mother's daughter instead of son, and the thought . . . causes

---
[5] Enck, p. 149.

me neither pain, fear nor embarrassment . . . I would not have matured into a muscular and self-willed Clytemnestra . . ."(1). More significant than the fact that Clytemnestra killed Cassandra is the fact that Skipper so willingly sees himself as female. Furthermore, it is in terms of Oedipus and Hamlet that Skipper tries to establish his identity, calling his father, wife, and daughter each "his own Antigone," and saying that "with Hamlet" he became Pixie's father(2). On a literal level, however, he feels that he is an "accomplice" to his father's death(7), and that his father's shot was meant for him(3). If we recall that he prefers the vision of his mother to his father's death, it can be concluded that this death occurred at a time when he construed it as an Oedipal victory over his father for his mother. The guilt he now feels for this, coupled with his mother's subsequent rejection, is central to his problem. The rejection dream itself is full of sexual image and symbol, such as the car's "thumping up and down, but silently" while the driver "grips a lever as tall and thin as a sword" and squeezes the "bulb," all of this occurring while the "sun" is "buried" in clouds and the "son" is hiding in the bushes(8-9). "I have always remained my mother's son"(98), he later admits, significantly.

The next relationship, chronologically, is that with his wife, Gertrude (note the connection with *Hamlet*), and is particularly underplayed in Skipper's narrative because it is his most patent failure as a man. Enough is told, however, to make it clear despite his desire to conceal. She clearly hates him ("I hope they sink you, Edward, I really do"[131]), supposedly had had "motorcycle orgies" with members of his own crew(130), and is said to have even made a "play for faithful Sonny(131)," this latter probably in an attempt to humiliate him more decisively than the other acts did. Surely she is aware of his impotency; the fact that she turned to other men may be a result of this. It may well be that she asks him, "at least you won't deny me hate, will you?"(131) because he had already denied her love. After her death, significantly by suicide at a motel of questionable reputation, their relationship is made clear by the highly important symbolism of the funeral and the sword. In the first place, he fails her even in death as he did sexually in life, arriving late for the interment and having trouble with his sword(130). Earlier he could not use it properly and needed Sonny's help with it, and at the funeral it is buried in her grave—a symbol buried symbolically in failure with the woman he had failed, and buried not by him, but by Sonny.

Death has a way of leading Skipper to new episodes in his search for love and self-justification. After his mother's death, he tries and fails with Gertrude, just as after her death he tries with Cassandra, to be followed later by Kate—each experience forcing him toward accepting his artificial potency on Sonny's island. The transfer of his search and affection from Gertrude to Cassandra is the most specific, for when they are leaving the cemetery, he tells her, "when we get home, Cassandra," shutting his eyes, "I want you to try on that camel's hair coat. I think her camel's hair coat might fit you, Cassandra"(135).

That he has incestuous desires for Cassandra seems to be clear. Not only does he very often admire the body of his "teen-age bomb"(32), but he often describes his enjoyment at caressing her and kissing her. At one point he even likens himself and Cassandra to Paris and Helen. It is clear that she is aware of this to some degree, for at the tattoo parlor, while he is thinking of her as "my child courtesan," she insists on sarcastically calling him "my boy friend"(16-17). Later, when Miranda is seducing him in the hot rod, he looks anxiously at the house for Cassandra, and Miranda says significantly, "Cassandra? Cassandra? Like mother, like daughter, isn't that about it? You and your poor little Candy Cane"(96). The only questions here are whether Skipper's "love" for her may be less incestual in fact than a form of over-compensation for his failures to her, or, as self-justification, another example of his unreliability.

An episode which similarly reveals his impotency and unreliability is that of the "kissin' bandits." Before they arrive, Skipper tells us, he had been "awake, alert, ready for anything," "the solitary sentinel"(38), yet he does nothing to defend Cassandra. He indirectly absolves himself by presenting them as having been fully equipped, in "full battle pack," with "rows of dangling hand grenades" and "unsheathed and flashing trench knives or bayonets"(41). The comedy in such a picture is apparent, but Skipper must show their "fierceness"(39) if he is to be forgiven for inaction. Because of his unreliability, he is distorting this entire picture just as he will do in the *Peter Poor* episode for the same reason, but the truth in both instances is there to be found. After the "kissin' " (a euphemism, surely—bandits have stripped naked just to kiss her?), the leader tells them to "make it count" and to "get rid of [their] eggs"(41), and they line up as Skipper urges courage. With the first man, Cassandra's "eyes were searching him and waiting"(42); with the second, she tries with "irritation" and "impatience"(43) to free her hand from Skipper's grasp; and with the third, she not only returns his kiss, but caresses him and whispers, "give me your gun, please"(43). Then, after the narrator's significant ellipsis, the soldiers are gone and Cassandra draws the pea jacket "into place once more"(43). Since Skipper had not been able to stop the rape, if that is not too strong a word, he will not admit that it took place.

The most revealing episode in Skipper's time of trials occurs on Miranda's island. It stands in such high relief in Skipper's mind that throughout the novel Miranda's story must wait—"hold your horses," he says(110). Indeed, she figures so prominently in his inadequacies that Skipper describes the Kate episode as his "triumph" over her(48). She is a "monster"(5) and his "enemy"(52) because she dominates him fearfully. He must either close his eyes while speaking to her(58) or "force himself" to return her stare(65). She drinks like a man(63), talks like a man(58), "could outrun horses on the beach"(64), and has a bosom like "an unleashed animal"(59). After their first encounter on the beach, he runs home "cold and sweating"(59); and when he sees her later in her home, she is in a "man's white shirt" and "sitting back on her heels—wicked posturing, rank mystery of the triangle"(62).

Later, when she tries unsuccessfully to seduce him in her car, another test he fails completely, she is simply frightening to him. "No snowballs," he pleads as they walk to the car(93), for, as will be shown below, snowballs were a part of an assault on his manhood also. Frightening to him also is the way she sits symbolically "ramming the clutch pedal in and out" in her impatience(94), with her "greater-than-life-size-breasts"(95). The gearshift lever that "rose up like a whip" has a death's head for a knob(94). He "wanted only to put [his] head between [his] knees, to cover [his] bare head with [his] arms and sleep"(94)—sleep again, and this time in the fetal position. Nevertheless, he feels "sick at last"(94) at the situation, and in the face of "desire and disaster"(96) he kicks himself free of her, out of the car, and into flight. "Burning. Blinded. But applauding [himself] for the escape"(96). (This central scene, incidentally, is one labelled as "simply ludicrous" in one review of the novel.)

The next attack occurs aboard the *Peter Poor*. Red and Jomo are able to carry out their planned assault on Cassandra without interference from Skipper, just as the soldiers did. It is this episode which most clearly establishes Skipper's unreliability as a narrator. He does not tell us that Cassandra had sexual relations while he was ineffectually lying asleep in the face of danger (in fact, he describes the scene in terms of innocent lunching and sailcraft instruction), but we learn that two months later a two-month old fetus is left for him by Cassandra through Miranda(190). Cassandra very pointedly demonstrates his impotence by forcing him to show Red the tattoo of Fernandez's name—an important symbol of his emasculation(188), as will be discussed below. After several years on the island with Kate and Sonny, incidentally, this tattoo "has all but disappeared"(47), but it is bright now.

The *Peter Poor* assault is foreshadowed in two scenes. At the dance, Skipper is unable to keep Red, Jomo, and Bub away from Cassandra; and they are seen "cutting in on each other, spitting on their hands" and showing "their dark design"(84). The snowball attack in the yard also foreshadows the *Peter Poor* test. The sexual nature of this attack is evident not only in the language used to describe it, such as "discharged," "patter," "spent"(88), but also more clearly in the fact that Skipper's first thought is "TREMLOW"(87). "Tremlow, come out and fight," he yells, and "swings" and "growls" at them, "helpless, wet and bleeding"(87). Could this, he wonders comically, be the activity of island "lovers?"(87). Then he accurately guesses that Jomo, his newest rival for Cassandra, is behind it(88). That he is right is made clear by Jomo's "panting and . . . trousers . . . sopping wet up to the knees"(88). In this scene we see for the first time that his daughter is aware of what is going on, if not a participant in it, but Skipper never hints at this in his narrative.

The hot rods on Miranda's island are further symbols of his impotence because, although they normally represent manliness (here they are described as having a "whip" of steel, thick "tubes," and as "throbbing" with power[78]), Skipper fails in every encounter with them. He is almost not allowed to ride *to* the dance, and when he does, must ride like a woman on a man's lap(79); he is not allowed to ride *from* the dance at all after his several failures(92); he fails in the hot rod with Miranda; and he fails in the hot rod race on the beach to catch Jomo and save Cassandra(195). Even he admits that "in Miranda's eyes [he] was not the man to win a hot rod race"(192). When he does drive the hot rod—in the drag race—he names his mount "Cicisbeo," significantly a *cavalier servente* of a married *woman*.

In the triangle Skipper and Cassandra form with Fernandez we find another clear example of Skipper's deception. He is "uncomfortable"(23) when asked what happened to Fernandez, even admitting later that "shadings of the true tonality were lost, and certain details were kept to [himself] "(149), and that he was "sparing" Cassandra "certain details, withholding others, failing somehow to convey the true tonality of the thing"(149). The question here is whether he has homosexual interest in Fernandez, and in view of his general unreliability, he may.[6] In establishing identities in the first chapter, he includes Fernandez in his "roster of persons whose love I have lost"(5). Also, before the wedding he describes Fernandez in bridal terms: "Skull that cried for lace and candlelight, in his jacket pocket a Bible bound in white calfskin, and in his hand . . . flowers"(4). In addition, he pats him on the knee(114), squeezes his hand(115), and wants the chance to welcome him with "opened arms"(5)—and that it is "opened" rather than "open" suggests more than the cliché meaning. Inasmuch as we learn later that Fernandez is referred to as "a little fairy"(157), it is safe to assume that Skipper knew it early, especially in view of the fact that he did everything in order to bring the marriage about in the first place. We know that he "was always afraid that Cassandra would marry a marine"(123)—a strong symbol of manliness. When we learn that Pixie had been born at seven and a half months, the reason she had married Fernandez may become as clear to us as it does to him before he renounces Skipper and his family(129). The reason for Skipper's pushing the marriage may become clearer also.

Their relationship may be seen from the beginning of the marriage. For

---

[6]It is worth noting that there are many implications in the novel that this is true. The color green, popularly emblematic of homosexuality, is spattered throughout the novel in just those scenes hinting of homosexuality in other ways. In Fernandez's case, for example, his guitar, the tattoo, and the car are all green. So are many things relating to the "kissin' bandits," the dance, the *Peter Poor* episode, the beach scenes, etc. Also, Skipper often describes his walk in feminine terms, and is very interested in feminine clothing and male bodies, especially Tremlow's and those of the "bandits." Finally, many other characters recognize his femininity, usually resulting in fine comedy. Miranda calls him an "old maid" and illustrates this by calling him the "Mah Jongg champion"; he is forced to sit on Bub's "tough wiry little lap"; the grandmother and Bubbles tease him about his appeal to women; etc.

example, the seating arrangement in the car not only has Fernandez seated next to Skipper, but at the opposite end of the seat from his bride(116). Then, too, the very fact of Skipper's being on the honeymoon is significant. The car is important as "somehow a desperate equivalent" of Fernandez(117), with its abnormal "battered" hood and "smashed-in" grille(113)— the male symbol mutilated. It should be noted the Fernandez is unable to drive this car, and Cassandra does so "only with the greatest effort and determination"(4); that on the trip Fernandez becomes flirtatious by coquettishly showing his legs and asking her if she likes "cheesecake"(119); and that he tells Skipper that "it will be a very short honeymoon, Papa Cue Ball, I assure you. A very short honeymoon." Skipper responds by smiling and admiring him(112). Perhaps as valuable is the symbolic water hose at the gas station "lashing about in a perverse and frenzied circle, lashing and taking aim and soaking the lower half of [Skipper's] fresh white uniform"(113).

The final evidence deserving of consideration in this relationship is the tattoo of Fernandez's name that Cassandra forces on Skipper. The suggestion of homosexuality makes this episode all the more meaningful. Skipper ironically submits to this "exquisite torture"(19) "only for Cassandra"(17); the color is bright green, and "green's going to hurt"(17); and Cassandra later describes Harry, the man for whose love Fernandez leaves, as a man who "was 'tattooed,' the whisper dying, dying, the mouth coming as close as it could to a smile, 'like you, Skipper' "(24). Later, when he tries to embrace her before the dance, she withdraws to "trace out" the tattoo while he thinks, "did she, could she know what she was doing? know the shame I felt for the secret I still kept from her?"(74). When considered together, these points reveal meanings that the deceptive Skipper wishes to conceal, but which Hawkes wants to make clear.

Perhaps the most damaging failure that Skipper has is at the feast of *cojones* that he shares with Fernandez(123). This most masculine meal, supposed to make a man potent and fertile, succeeds only in making Skipper vomit. This is not only the wrong physical reaction, but it is the wrong emotional reaction. Skipper feels not passionate, but nauseated.

In the scene in Cassandra's bedroom after the near-seduction, nearly every symbol of Skipper's impotence in the novel appears in one paragraph(97). He has just come from Miranda's hot rod. He finds the crucifix in his pocket—the crucifix he had won in the "perverse" and "obscene" (and comic) belly-bumping contest with Uncle Billy(89), who had "never been on a woman" and had "never had a woman on [him]"(91). Skipper had won by suggesting at an opportune moment that Billy had bumped bellies with his mother(91). He had, therefore, won a contest of questionable masculinity from an admittedly asexual opponent by unfair means smacking of incest, but he keeps and uses the prize as a sign of his masculinity. Nevertheless, he places this crucifix on the dressmaker's dummy which Cassandra had dressed in his uniform "so that the artificial bosom swelled [his] white tunic and the artificial pregnancy of the padded belly puffed out the broad front of [his] . . . white duck pants which she had pinned to the dummy with a pair of giant safety pins rammed through the belt"(67). He naturally refers to this magnificently complex symbol as "that hapless effigy of my disfigured self"(67). He next finds the footwarmer which he used in the evening for "warming Cassandra's bed"(71), and which he empties "down the john"(72) in the morning, filled with water and "frozen solid"(97), and we see him standing in the bathroom with the bedwarmer "hanging cold and heavy from [his] hand"(72), totally useless for either act described. As he sets this outside the door, he thinks of Jomo's words of incantation, "blue tit," which gave "substance, body, to the dark color and falling temperature of [his] lonely and sleepless nights"(71), or his impotence. Finally, he remembers the prayer (written in green) "sleep with a gentle thought"—the highly ironic prayer he uses as "a talisman against the horrors of blue tit" and which "saved" him "from the thought of the black brassiere"(73), the symbol of his impotence with Miranda. This prayer, in other words, had helped him to deceive himself about his impotence.

It is his new life with its new and final set of relationships that enables Skipper to accept his impotence and live at peace. He has stopped trying to be what he is not; and he has masked his former failures with his second skin of deception. He has told his story in two parallel strands so as to explain away his failure and impotence while emphasizing his successes in the new life. He now lives with his beloved Sonny in triumph over Miranda and Cassandra because "there are many people who wish nothing more than to kiss him," and he names them: "Sonny! Catalina Kate!"(50). Previously he had likened Cassandra to the Blessed Virgin Mary—particularly when she was sexually in danger, as on the honeymoon trip(117), with the soldiers(42), and in the lighthouse(197)—while thinking her in part responsible for her fate each time(42, 175, 176). Now he feels triumph over her almost as though she were an enemy like Miranda. This may be due to her having been in competition with Sonny for his affections whether she knew it or not. From the first, Skipper was always the "lover of poor dear black Sonny"(1), who, back when Gertrude had made a play for him, had remained "faithful." On the ship, too, his "reverence was not all for God"(140). Later, when he is leaving Skipper and Cassandra to return to his island, Sonny damns "all unfaithful lovers" and says, "that unfaithful stuff is the devil! Pure devil!" Skipper's reaction is that "the shaft goes to the breast, love shatters, whole troop trains of love are destroyed"(24). He is the unfaithful lover of Sonny, and, after he gives Sonny the photographs of the *Starfish*, Sonny says, "maybe we ain't so busted up after all" (22), then "shines his black love into [Skipper's] heart" during their talk of the future(25). The final farewell is a crying, bumping, hugging, and kissing affair with Skipper blubbering all over Sonny, and although certainly comic, is an accurate picture of their relationship.

Now that they are living together—and note that they live together apart from Catalina Kate—their relationship is nothing if not stronger, more intimate. After looking at naked Sonny and delivering a poetic description of his body(102), he walks to the end of the barn "where Oscar the bull was watching [them]. 'What's the matter, Oscar,' [he] said, 'jealous of my attentions? Don't be jealous, Oscar,' [he] said softly, 'your time will come' "(105). The clear implication here is that there *is* something to be jealous about.

Sonny's role is more complex than just that of friend and lover, however. Just as Josie "vicariously shares the joys of pregnancy"(49) with Kate, so too does Skipper vicariously share with Sonny the joys of impregnating her. That Sonny is intimate with Kate is clear from the scene where they are lying on the grass at the picnic. As Sonny begins to pet her, Skipper thinks he should admonish with her, "hugging is all right, Kate, but nothing more. . . . You mustn't hurt the baby," but a few lines later he falls asleep without having said anything. Later, through his "half-sleep," he sees her washing Sonny's drawers in the spring(169). There is also no doubt that the baby is Sonny's, either. We often hear in the novel that Sonny is very black and Skipper is white. The baby is "three times as black" as Kate(209), and would not be if Skipper were the father. Furthermore, he never refers to the child as "mine," but as "for Sonny and me"(206). He asks her, "who do you think it looks like, Kate, Sonny or me?"(209) and tells her that "we can start you off on another little baby in a few weeks"(209). It should also be remembered that the gift of the hot dogs was for "Sonny and myself" and that Sonny "accepted [them] on behalf of both of us"(49). Here, again, as he had "helped the old man with his sword, and . . . can help [Skipper] with it"(130), Sonny is the active agent.

There remains but one step more for Skipper to take. The crucifix which he has kept as a symbol of manliness (though a false one) for seven years(100), and has carried with him on his insemination trips along with, and of equal importance with, the black bag, is most significantly given to Kate after the celebration party for their triumph(209). In this act is the sign of his acceptance of impotence; he has gained as much as he can expect to gain and is content to live in what love and peace he can find. He no longer needs the symbol to be happy, especially here on Sonny's island where his impotence is never tested and he is at least artificially potent.

"How different [a profession] from my morbid father's. And haven't I redeemed his profession . . . with my own?"(47), he asks. From dealing in the "seeds of death"(161) in the old life with "Father, Mother, Gertrude, Fernandez, Cassandra"(161) he turns to "seeds of life"(167) in the mystical "spell" of his new art and life. Skipper is careful to make his narrative structure emphasize this change. It is indeed significant that he take his new family (not the least important of whom is Sonny) to a graveyard to celebrate the birth of the child, for this is the triumph—the physical triumph—of life over death that is being marked. Here is at least one aspect of Hawkes' message of hope. The comic that he claims for the novel is self-evident. The only question about Skipper's "naked history" (and it is especially ironic that he has tried to *hide* rather than *expose* the truth about his history) is whether the price—self-deception—is not too much to pay for the artificiality of not only the insemination of both the cows and Kate, but of the artificiality of his newfound peace of mind based on this deception—this second skin.[7]

Albert J. Guerard

Second Skin: The Light and Dark Affirmation

Second Skin is the richest and most ambitious of John Hawkes's novels since *The Cannibal,* and without doubt the warmest and most genial. Inevitably it is a more vulnerable book than the tight, clipped, spare *The Beetle Leg* and *The Lime Twig:* such is one price of "letting go." Instead of *The Beetle Leg*'s parody (western Waste Land and Inferno) and *The Lime Twig*'s concentrated vision of the underground life, we have now a "mature" book frankly if still playfully dealing with large issues. The very largest ones, in fact—of how to be and how to go on living in the face of private catastrophe. A serene *Tempest,* the tempest tamed by art, dealing with our normal human ailments (regression, dread of castration, incest, etc.) in the consolingly familiar world of fairytale and myth. Spinning wheel and black witch, a small dragon on a wandering island. . . .

Second Skin is clearly a more accessible novel than the earlier ones; the number of printings and the near-won National Book Award are well deserved. It seems to have a particular appeal for good college students, who in the same breath will praise the awesome *Under the Volcano.* A paradox? Yet both novels, using quite different methods, express a great deal of feeling often left hidden or even undiscovered. Material that was muted, disguised or

---

[7]This paper was read at the Symposium on American Novelists at the 1968 Conference of the Pennsylvania Council of Teachers of English at Penn State in October, 1968.
Albert J. Guerard is professor of English at Stanford University.

actually repressed in the earlier Hawkes novels rises to the surface, only slightly displaced or not displaced at all. There is the psychic relief of having "things"—*i.e.,* ultimate anxieties—out in the open. But there is also, to mitigate darkness, Skipper's determined cheerfulness. A Caribbean version of pastoral! The final chapter begins with a parody of one of Dickens's cozy endings. "And didn't Sister Josie and Big Bertha pitch right in and help? Down on their hands and knees with the coconut fibers? And didn't I forbid Kate to have our baby in the swamp, and didn't Kate, young Catalina Kate, bear the baby on the floor of my own room in Plantation House and sleep with the sweat and pleasure of this her first attempt at bearing a baby for me—for Sonny and for me—in my own swaying hammock filled with flowers?" (Parody not only of language? Sexual "sharing," just beneath Dickens's consciousness in *Bleak House,* is here celebrated in a happy ending and dream of triangular bliss.)

Overtness, as always, renders art more accessible: sometimes the worst art, occasionally, as here, the best. Hawkes makes a very clear affirmative statement of theme. *Second Skin* is a vision of the will to survive death and abomination and of the power to move from impotence to fertility. "From the frozen and crunchy cow paths of the Atlantic island—my mythic rock in a cold sea—to the soft pageant through leaf, tendril, sun, wind, how far I had come." The wandering timeless Caribbean island is a place for *le bonheur,* the home of natural teeming life, "spongy and dense and saturated," though even Paradise has its reptiles. Skipper's narrative is serpentine; but snakes and lizards must be exorcised, and an iguana of monstrous proportions overcome.

How closely intertwined are the bright vision and the dark materials! Even Cassandra has a golden snake at the cleft of her throat and is, like Christabel, "serpentine in the moonlight." The wind, roaring across the island, is a "bundle of invisible snakes." "These snakes that fly in the wind are as large around as tree trunks; but pliant, as everlastingly pliant, as the serpents that crowd my dreams." The naked AWOL soldiers, violators of Cassandra in the desert, are lizards. The second skin (habiliment of Skipper's brave new Caribbean life) is also the translucent skin shed by snakes, in turn associated with the rubber of a contraceptive device. A very complex play of imagery (surrounding fears of impotence, castration, homosexual violation) juxtaposes snakes and rubber with the stinging of needles and of bees. Artificial bees sting at a moment of homosexual violation (displaced onto professional tattooing); and beehives are laboring inside Miranda's "enormous chest" in an hour of dreadful heterosexual threat. Scattered through the novel at crucial intervals are empty or wrecked nests.

Bees and serpents, immemorial creatures as familiar as the classic names—Cassandra, Miranda, Gertrude. Skipper might seem a doomed descendant of the house of Atreus. The initial trauma of the father's suicide is relived, through what Hawkes calls "chordal insistence," in the suicide of his wife and daughter, and in the murder and mutilation of his son-in-law. Three of the darkest moments are crowded together in a single chapter, "The Brutal Act." The mutiny on the *Starfish* and homosexual violation by Tremlow significantly follows a dance in which the rapist wears a grass skirt, a costume as sinister as the metallic vest of Larry the Limousine in *The Lime Twig.* The murdered son-in-law Fernandez has left behind castanets and a long white tasseled shawl. A victim of homosexual entrapment, he is as a result the victim of a smashing and of mutilation, losing all five fingers of the left hand. The scene echoes a more playful mutilation in *The Beetle Leg* and a total smashing in *The Lime Twig,* one that quite annihilated identity. This time the violence is very much out in the open, an almost realist notation of horror, the censorships and displacements very slight. The chapter returns at last to the child's effort, by playing the cello, to thwart his father's suicide—a four-page scene interestingly amplified in Hawkes's play, *The Undertaker.* The trauma is responsible, we there see at some length, for infantilism and regression.

Dark materials, overcome by Skipper's engaging voice, by style and novelistic art. The northern island (which I associate incorrigibly with the Vinalhaven of Hawkes's cool foggy summers, as the other island with Grenada where he wrote the book) is a fit counterpart to the maimed, stunted bleak Germany of *The Cannibal,* and it is pleasing to see the chicken strangled in that novel here restored to life. (Chickens, phallic creatures that they are, easily strangled or decapitated, or violently stimulated as in *The Day of the Locust,* have a particularly wretched time in anti-realist fiction from the time of Lautréamont!) The paragraph of Puritan bleakness appropriately concludes with an image of denied life:

> . . . The larch trees with their broken backs, the enormous black sky streaked with fistfuls of congealed fat, the abandoned Poor House that looked like a barn, the great brown dripping box of the Lutheran church bereft of sour souls, bereft of the hymn singers with poke bonnets and sunken and accusing horse faces and dreary choruses, a few weather-beaten cottages unlighted and tight to the dawn and filled, I could see at a glance, with the marvelous dry morality of calico and beans and lard, and then a privy, a blackened pile of tin cans, and even a rooster, a single live rooster strutting in a patch of weeds and losing his broken feathers, clutching his wattles, every moment or two trying to crow into the wind, trying to grub up the head of a worm with one of his snubbed-off claws, cankerous little bloodshot rooster pecking away at the dawn in the empty yard of some dead fisherman. . . . Oh, it was all spread before me and all mine, the strange island of bitter wind and blighted blueberries and empty nests. (55)[1]

---

[1] *Second Skin* (New York: New Directions, 1964).

The wandering southern island, by contrast, is a place of teeming pullulant life. "The ants were racing through the holes in my tennis shoes and the tide was a rhythmic darkening of the sand and something was beating great frightened wings in the swamp." Skipper accepts with love rather than disgust the bovine serenity of Catalina Kate, and the fact that she is shared by his mess-boy Sonny—a dream transcending racial and sexual barriers. And Skipper loves too his new profession as artificial inseminator of cows. No longer the passive victim of tattooist, the instrument this time in his own mouth, he is expert "in soft dalliance transplanting the bull and stopping the tide of the heifer." The passage, perhaps honorably indebted to Isaac Snopes's poetic affair with a cow, is an uninhibited consecration of the natural, though the act is "artificial." "As for a blackbird sitting on a cow's rump, there surely is the perfect union, the meeting of the fabulous herald and the life source":

> . . . And I was opposite from Sonny and knew just what to do, just how to do it—reaching gently into the blind looking glass with my eye on the blackbird on Sonny's cap—and at the very moment that the loaded pipette might have disappeared inside, might have slipped from sight forever, I leaned forward quickly and gave a little puff into the tube—it broke the spell, in a breath lodged Oscar firmly in the center of the windless unsuspecting cave that would grow to his presence like a new world and void him, one day, onto the underground waters of the mysterious grove—and pulled back quickly, slapped her rump, tossed the flexible spent pipette in the direction of the satchel and grinned as the whole tree burst into the melodious racket of the dense tribe of blackbirds cheering for our accomplished cow. (171)

Always defeated, and with a cemetery his "battleground," Skipper appears ultimately to triumph, and the birth of the baby is celebrated with a picnic in a cemetery, on the night of All Saints: a culminating equanimity. Is the younger middle-aged Hawkes going soft, as Conrad undeniably went soft and at last even Faulkner, the mysogyny attenuated and the tragic vision denied? Hardly, or at least "not yet," since the underground terrors are so marvelously vivid. The essential Hawkesian wry absurdity remains, and much of the tough intensity of language, even though life has, it would seem, been "accepted." Moreover, there are familiar dark pleasures to connect *Second Skin* with the earlier macabre visions. The iconography of vaguely obscene dance, playful surrogate for unsatisfactory sex, reappears in the belly-bumping contest on the northern island. Significantly, Skipper wins this contest while Cassandra is taken outside, a helpless victim. The first violation of Cassandra occurs in a scene that characteristically juxtaposes the violent and the everyday. Skipper must watch impotently the three naked soldiers' mechanical, methodical assault while the safe world of the Greyhound bus is only a few feet away.

The scene is in every respect more frightening because the rapes are described as kisses. "And Pinocchio's kiss: foam, foam, foam!" Partial Freudian displacement, displacement that has become conscious and even comically recognizable, remains powerful precisely because the symbolic acts are themselves terrifying. Incisions and smashings and tattooings evoke their own primitive fears whatever they may "symbolize," not to mention iguanas stuck to the back. Such displacements and transformations are the joys of grotesque art in any age. But perhaps the closest analogue to Hawkes's practice is to be found in the *Chants de Maldoror* of Lautréamont (a writer so appalled by his own comic darkness, as it happens, that he "went soft" almost immediately, and embraced sweetness and light with real violence).

The symbolic methods of *Second Skin* are thus less obfuscated than in the earlier novels, and the anxieties themselves more overt. But they are also more complicated. Sexual "materials" (his own word) are absolutely central in Hawkes's work. But it is well to remember that they are materials for elaborated comic fiction and for "art." One should not read *Second Skin* for psychological information; on the other hand the reader may well find there that glimpse of truth for which he has forgotten to ask. An unusually elaborate configuration intensifies unusually explicit forbidden longings as well as mortal fears. There is nothing in the least secret about Skipper's love for his daughter Cassandra, his "teen-age bomb" and teasing Lolita. He accompanies her on her honeymoon, sits in the car between bride and groom, and enjoys at last having "an excuse" to examine her purse and its contents. The ludicrous Freudian activity, which Conrad might have imagined in all innocence, is quite conscious in Hawkes. Earlier in the book, though later in time, the tattooing incident offers appalling complications. Skipper is tattooed across the chest not with the name of his mother, gentle Mildred, but (at Cassandra's insistence) with the name of the dead son-in-law, Fernandez. The stinging needles, those artificial bees, evoke a "strenuous black bat" struggling in a bloated mouth (a repugnant act of fellatio?) and eventually a "sudden recall of what Tremlow had done to me that night—helpless abomination . . ."

There is a recurring voyeuristic pattern, accompanied by regression to childhood and even infancy. Perhaps significantly, Skipper recalls his degradation by Tremlow shortly before the three AWOL soldiers appear near the disabled bus. The three men who crawl up the embankment are deadly lizards waiting to strike; they glisten "like watery sardines." Skipper can do no more than squeeze Cassandra's hand by way of urging her to be brave, squeeze "for dear life and in all my protective reassurance and slack alarm." The violation of Cassandra on the *Peter Poor,* with Skipper once again a helpless bystander, involves much business with rubber boots and oilskins. Skipper, struggling to put on this second skin, is indeed back in early childhood: ". . . felt my cheeks puffing out under the flaps of the little tight preposterous sou'wester, felt the chin strap digging in."

We are much closer than before, on the *Peter Poor,* to a true primal scene, with Skipper formally excluded, locked off from the successful lovers. He makes his effort to break in on them and is knocked back. Before falling asleep or passing out, he becomes aware of a rubber hip boot that fell onto his stomach and "lay there wet and flapping and undulating on my stomach." The very act and process of displacement is here dramatized, the physical movement and change of boot to penis. The disorderly cabin, symbolic of sexual turmoil, is as charged as one of Conrad's Malayan jungles in the early novels.[2] May we hazard, amid much other interesting confusion, that the triangle of voyeuristic father-daughter-intruding male seems to be a substitute for the classic family of voyeuristic son-mother-father?

Skipper's psychological regression, true; yet an authorial recapturing of the child's gift for fantasy and, even, a Dickensian child's view of the world. In his critical commentary written for *The Personal Voice* Hawkes speaks of the

> . . . elemental fears and desires, which are constants in the inner lives of men. Fear of the unknown, fear of sexual destruction at the hands of the father, fear of annihilation at the hands of absolute authority, infantile desire for the security and sublimity of the mother's love—these components of the familiar Oedipal situation as defined by Freud are to be found in significant literature through the ages. Such literature tells us that the adult's life is never completely removed from the life of the child, but that whether we achieve self-fulfillment or suffer spiritual death often depends on our ability or inability to return to forgotten experience and to uncover again the powerful emotional energies of childhood.[3]

Elsewhere in the same essay Hawkes says that, for the contemporary writer, "the liberating processes of the imagination may result in his discovery of characters closely resembling the heroes, benevolent guides, destructive demons, or awe-inspiring gods that we find in myths, dreams, fantasies, and fairy tales." *Second Skin,* like much of Dickens at his best, conveys at times a child's visual world (both grotesque and magnified) as well as childish fears. Lured outdoors from the high school dance, Skipper experiences the brutal snowballing as a child would, though he suddenly sees Tremlow as again the

---

[2] . . . I fell around facing the cabin and managed to hold myself upright with one hand still on the ladder.

Pots and pans and beer bottles were rolling around on the floor. Two narrow bunks were heaped high with rough tumbled blankets and a pair of long black rubber hip boots. Little portholes were screwed tightly shut, the exhaust of the gasoline engine was seeping furiously through a leaking bulkhead, and in front of me, directly in front of me and hanging down from a hook and swaying left and right, a large black lace brassiere with enormous cups and broad elasticized band and thin black straps was swaying right and left from a hook screwed into the cabin ceiling.

[3] Edited by Albert J. Guerard, Maclin B. Guerard, John Hawkes, Claire Rosenfield (New York: Lippincott, 1964). The second sentence quoted does not appear in the shorter paperback edition of this anthology.

antagonist, "the ringleader of my distant past." The sandwich on the bus is magnified, mysterious, ghostly. The drawing of three glasses of beer, during the honeymoon, similarly returns us to a child's world of glittering eyes and enormous size, and a silver hairless dog that tips its sharp trembling ears at him. Very pure Dickens, that hairless dog! And tortillas served in the same spooky cafe, with its cash register looking like "a cranky medieval machine of death"? The tortillas are filled with "tiny black explosive seeds" and tortured, lacerated chicken; they bring the pain of unleashed fire. The preserved vegetables are "poisoned in such a way as to bring a sudden film to the eyes and pinched dry shriveling sensations to the nose and throat."

This has a familiar Dickensian explicitness and insistence. Rather more interesting are those scenes in which the primitive animating power is not explained at all. In *The Lime Twig* Hencher, luxuriating in a regression to childhood, prepares breakfast to serve his surrogate parents in bed. Outside the kitchen window gulls hover strangely. But, stranger still, one gull follows when he goes into the bedroom and beats its wings against the window. A bird stranger than, for instance, Robbe-Grillet's gull precisely because we do not hear of it again. A comparable bird appears in *Second Skin,* in a paragraph loaded with imageries of childish fear. The yarn dangling from Cassandra's wrists is a "black umbilicus" and lives "in the cave of Miranda's sewing bag." A black entanglement and true Dickensian intensity:

> Shanks of ice hanging from the eaves, the wind sucking with increasing fury at the wormholes, Miranda standing in the open front doorway and laughing into the wind or bellowing through the fog at her two fat black Labradors and throwing them chunks of meat from a galvanized iron basin slung under her arm, the ragged bird returning each dawn to hover beyond the shore line outside my window, empty Grand Dad bottles collecting in the kitchen cupboards, under the stove, even beside the spinning wheel in the parlor—so these first weeks froze and fled from us, and Cassandra grew reluctant to explore the cow paths with me, and my nights, my lonely nights, were sleepless. I began to find the smudged saucers everywhere—stink of the asthma powders, stink of secret designs and death—and I began to notice that Cassandra was Miranda's shadow, sweet silent shadow of the big widow in slacks. (69)

The name of Dickens, whom Hawkes much admires, may give pause. Yet a biographer might well discover in Hawkes the same perverse taste and talent for administration doubling an inner life of wayward fantasy. And, incidentally, the same talent for incantatory public speaking. Two other eminent names suggest new elements of accessibility in *Second Skin*: Vladimir Nabokov and Saul Bellow. To say this is not to affirm influence, but only an occasional analogous impulse. The deepest Hawkesian voice of the earlier novels remains intact; so too the familiar ironic and distorting imagination. But these sometimes work, at the surface, in new manners or "styles."

The opening chapter is written in very beautiful, supple, deliberately rhythmed and quite "traditional" prose. To mention Nabokov is to note chiefly, perhaps, the suave relishing of words and rhythms: a prose of delicate balances. The impressionist mode, with its controlled wandering of memory and nuanced foreshadowing of later incidents, supports a conventional but exquisitely managed first-person narration. So we have, at the outset, a subduing of chaos, almost a formal invocation. The elaborate reasonings and even the composed classical allusions reach us through what is, still, a speaking voice:

> Had I been born my mother's daughter instead of son—and the thought is not so improbable, after all, and causes me neither pain, fear nor embarrassment when I give it my casual and interested contemplation—I would not have matured into a muscular and self-willed Clytemnestra but rather into a large and innocent Iphigenia betrayed on the beach. A large and slow-eyed and smiling Iphigenia, to be sure, even more full to the knife than that real girl struck down once on the actual shore. Yet I am convinced that in my case I should have been spared. All but sacrified I should have lived, somehow, in my hapless way; to bleed but not to bleed to death would have been my fate, forgiving them all while attempting to wipe the smoking knife on the bottom of my thick yellow skirt. Or had my own daughter been born my son I would have remained his ghostly guardian, true to his hollow cheeks and skinny legs and hurts, for no more than this braving his sneers, his nasty eye and the scorn of his fellow boys. For him too I would have suffered violence with my chin lifted, my smile distracted, my own large breast the swarming place of the hummingbirds terrified and treacherous at once. (1-2)

I can think of no Nabokovian moment precisely like this, yet seem to recognize a kindred assurance and kindred power to compose memory, as well as a suavity of style. So too the vision of Skipper's mother as still alive, still living in a Proustian eternal present, evokes both the beauties of *Speak, Memory* and the fine story of Delmore Schwartz, "In Dreams Begin Responsibilities."

The reminder of Saul Bellow is on the whole less pleasing. For there are times when Hawkes, in the very manner of Bellow, seems to seek intensity through the staccato crowding of vivid and clever details, a "writer" straining for "effects":

> But on flowed Cassandra, small, grave, heartless, a silvery water front adventuress, and led me straight into the crawling traffic—it was unlighted, rasping, a slow and blackened parade of taxicabs filled with

moon-faced marines wearing white braid and puffing cherry-tipped cigars, parade of ominous jeeps each with its petty officer standing up in the rear, arms folded, popping white helmets strapped in place. . . . (15)

Or,

Only the flare burning where we had left the road and now the scent of a lone cigarette, the flick of a match, the flash of a slick comb through bay rum and black waves of hair, persistent disappointed sounds of the ukelele—devilish hinting for a community sing—only the cooling sand of the high embankment against which Cassandra and Pixie and I huddled while the sailors grew restless and the driver—puttees, goggles, snappy cap and movements of ex-fighter-pilot, fierce nigger carefully trained by the Greyhound line—bustled about the enormous sulphuric round of the tire. (36)

There is no "personal voice" here (or there are too many voices), perhaps because more than one perceiving mind is at work.[4] Similarly disturbing at times is the effort, so familiar in Bellow, to present, in the same narrator, slack street-corner slang and a gift for poetry, incisive simile, metaphor. The language of Augie March at times, and often of Henderson, does not correspond to any recognizable personality . . . though all of us have known, of course, the English professor peppering his metaphorical *trouvailles* with gutter slang and four-letter words: tough masculine talk for a hairy-chested role. Skipper confronted by Sonny and Kate, or by the iguana, evokes some of the awkwardness of Henderson addressing native chiefs or in symbolic converse with the lion: " 'Well, Kate,' I said, and let go, stood up, wiped my brow, 'it looks as if he's there for good. Got us licked, hasn't he, Kate? Licked from the start. He means to stay right where he is until he changes his mind and crawls off under his own power. So the round goes to the dragon, Kate. I'm sorry.' "

Few creative problems are more teasing for the modern American writer than this one: how to toughen the literary language without impoverishing it, how to escape mandarin sinuosities without sacrificing richness. It is doubtless to Hawkes's credit that he should attempt at least briefly to write, with Bellow and Mailer, a muscularly "American" poetic prose. But of the two relatively new tonalities to appear in *Second Skin*, I find the supple and suave one more pleasing: the voice magisterially controlling the chaos it has remembered and evoked. The novel ends, very appropriately, in quietness:

---

[4]It cannot be emphasized too strongly that a writer's "voice" derives largely from his rhythms of thought, whether accelerated or leisurely, whether abrupt in transition or slowly modulated.

So yesterday the birth, last night the grave, this morning the baby in my arms—I gave Uncle Billy's crucifix to Kate this morning. I thought she deserved it—and this afternoon another trip to the field because Gloria was calling, calling for me. And now? Now I sit at my long table in the middle of my loud wandering night and by the light of a candle—one half-burned candle saved from last night's spectacle—I watch this final flourish of my own hand and muse and blow away the ashes and listen to the breathing among the rubbery leaves and the insects sweating out the night. Because now I am fifty-nine years old and I knew I would be, and now there is the sun in the evening, the moon at dawn, the still voice. That's it. The sun in the morning. The moon at dawn. The still voice. (209-210)

Second Skin, all in all, is the culmination (for the moment) of a slow and often conscious process of change and "development"—from the deep dynamic disturbed and utterly original vision of *The Cannibal* (where the pressure of still concealed or repressed fantasies had a marked effect on language and plot) to the absolutely expert, controlled and conscious use of myth and fairy story in *Second Skin,* and to its exploitation, at once terrifying and wonderfully comic, of menacing sexual materials. This seems to me on the whole a more important movement than the evident progress toward "realism," though there is doubtless some relationship between the two. There is obviously danger in a highly original writer becoming conscious of his own methods—the danger of self-imitation, of course, but also the danger of alarmed self-repudiation, as with Lautréamont.

It is now apparent, however, that Hawkes will always be strange enough—and restless enough. At forty-five he offers the consoling example of a major writer rather than an eccentric innovator: one determined to explore both the inherited resources of the novel form and those he has, in some sense, invented himself.